THE

EKBALLISt

A Novella

GP HAGGART

"Who knows what evil lurks in the hearts of men? The Shadow knows."

- *The Shadow*

Exorcism: From the Greek word, "exorkizo", and means to extract the demonic by an oath, formula or ritual. Scripturally, this term is only used in relation to the demonic to describe the sons of Sceva's work (Acts 19:13).

Ekballism: From the Greek word "ekballo", which means to eject, pluck out, or send away demons with a word or presence. This term is command-driven, and not dependent upon a formula or ritual.

"Verily, verily, I say unto you, He that believeth on me, the works that I do shall he do also; and greater works than these shall he do; because I go unto my Father."

John 14:12

content

DEDICATION

This book is dedicated to glorify God and to give Him thanks for helping me through it all.

THE WITCH GIRL

A breeze whipped up and hit the trees along the street, causing leaves to lose their footing and get caught in the air. The leaves slowly descended down onto the street where they were swept up by smaller breezes. Some of them stayed on the street while others were brushed up onto lawns. A car drives by and the leaves are captured again in the drifts made by the car. I sat in my truck enjoying the quiet of the cab and watching the winds catch the leaves and move them. I wait for my friend while he retrieves some of his things from a friend of his. Ben was a Christian rap artist and evangelist, working with several ministries in the area. We met through my church's youth pastor, Wil, who was also a Christian rap artist. The two of them liked to rap on the street while a group of us ministers got together to do some street preaching.

Ben had surprised me when the passenger door quickly opened and he hoped in. He had a tendency when someone came to visit him or when going out to do ministry work, to have the person with a car escort him around. Thinking we were done with his rounds we made one more stop at his place of work and he was finally contacted by Wil, who said that he would meet us at the house. We were heading over to a home where Ben and Wil claimed evil spirits were haunting a family of a mother and her two daughters. The mother was worried that the spirits would harm her oldest daughter's new born. Her youngest daughter made new friends whose mother was a witch practicing magick. When she would visit her new friends she was being influenced by their mother on the magical arts. Upon coming home she would practice witchcraft in secret places of the home. Ben and Wil informed me that she was caught practicing Wicca and other occult media and when they were asked by the mother to talk with her they investigated the home using discernment and they both felt that there was three evil spirits in the home. But the most interesting thing that the both of them told me was the periods of possession the girl went through and how she would write on the walls in her bedroom. The young witch had painted her walls black and the molding red. She would take paint, chalk and white marker and write on the walls various sayings and phrases. I wanted to see it but was rather fearful of what I might encounter even when I would meet the young girl.

Ben and Wil had asked me to check their case out before the mother would consider talking to the local Catholic parish priest. We had no problems with the Catholic Church we just considered ourselves Protestant and felt that the family would have to go through a lot of red tape with the Catholic Church before they would get delivered from the evil.

Ben and Wil had minor experience with evil spirits working with Pastor Bill who ran a local evangelism ministry traveling around the state, city to city, trying to fill church pews. Bill was a mentor of mine and I nickname him PB&J as a joke. He was the most loving man I ever knew and used to be a state correctional officer until he saw the resurrected Christ, quit his job and began saving souls for Christ. Many called him apostle due to seeing Jesus and being called to ministry. I swear no one could make him mad except for the devil. When the devil would show up Bill got righteously angry and would cast out what ever demons were about. Since I met him he inspired me to wear a collar for the whole purpose that people would quickly respect me and know where I came from; especially since I was a new bishop at the time.

Bill wasn't around at the time to cast out the evil spirits in the home so Ben and Wil, knowing of my first encounter with a demon, asked me if I could cast the spirits out. I was a little taken back at first but agreed after realizing that this may have been a divine appointment that God was setting up. I knew of divine appointments when my old mentor Pastor Dwayne was helping me through my first experience. He taught me so much about how the devil works and how demons operate. There was also Pastor Jim who helped me to understand what happened to me and counseled me through the painful memories and nightmares. All of my mentors told me that I would eventually have to deal with demons again because I was touched by them. When Ben and Wil asked me to look at their case I was hesitant at first. I really didn't want to go down that path again. However, there was a part of me that often wondered what a demon would say to me after all these years since my experience. I worried if I was ready to deal with the mental trauma again should something happen. Nevertheless, I felt God was calling me to help this family so I agreed because part of me wanted some pay back on the devil for what he did to me.

We arrived at the house and I quickly noticed that it was a duplex. I had wondered if that would cause a problem; and quickly realized how easy it would be for a family to suffer through a haunting in a duplex if a family of occultists lived next door. Knowing the occult world all too well since I use to be an occultist in my youth; I knew the tricks that occultist could do that would cause harm on others. I would discover in later cases that involved duplexes that it can be rather difficult to remove evil spirits since there are basically two families living in the same house but separate.

We entered the home and I was greeted by the oldest daughter. From the kitchen out came the witch girl who was dressed in jeans and a t-shirt. She spotted me and I saw her eyes move down to my collar and she quickly went upstairs. I moved over and sat on the couch, remaining quit and listened to Ben and Wil's conversation with the oldest daughter. She informed us that their mother was working and couldn't get out of work to meet with us so she was in charge. She was of elder age, appearing to be in her twenties. I usually felt uncomfortable being alone with another woman and the idea of three men and two girls in a house together didn't sit well with me. However, the oldest had informed us that she was in her mid-twenties but the youngest was fourteen. I understood that Wil knew the mother well to understand that there wouldn't be any worries on her end.

I was invited to look around the house so I got up and as soon as I did the youngest daughter came down stairs and appeared completely different. She wore cut up black pants, a revealing shirt and gothic makeup. She had placed black lip stick on her lips and colored her nails black. She wore a metal upright pentagram around her neck and pierced ears. We were all very surprised that she changed so quickly and her appearance made us all feel uncomfortable. Wil was quick to be the critic since he knew the girls' mother and requested her to go back upstairs and change into something more appropriate. She refused and left into another room. I walked about the house entering the basement and attempting to use the gift of discernment to try and locate any spirits in the home. Mysteriously I wasn't able to discern anything in the home and didn't know what to think of it all. I went up the stairs and into the kitchen then made my way to the top floor as Ben led me. He pointed to the room with the writing on the walls then he left back down stairs. I walked into the room and saw the black walls and red molding they told me about. At first I thought that young girl had some psychological issues but then noticed that the writing was different. The writing appeared to come from different people; no two hand writings were the same. As I turned to walk out of the room the young witch appeared in front of me and asked how I liked her work. I glanced at her to notice her eyes were widened and staring at me. Hesitating at first, I replied that it was interesting, then walked around her and made my way downstairs. I sat back down on the couch and said a silent prayer and waited for guidance from the Holy Spirit. I was hungry. I hadn't had anything to eat since I got up in the morning. I planned to fast and pray until the work of the Lord was over in this house, but couldn't wait to get out of the home and be on my way and find a fast food place. However, I shut out that voice that was crying out to being greedy. It was that part of my soul called the flesh that the Apostle Paul described in Galatians chapter five. The flesh wanted things badly and if not controlled would rule a person's life. I knew from my training in deliverance ministry that we needed to pray and fast for this purpose, to keep our flesh in check and allow our spirit to come out more to better hear from God. Freud would call the flesh the Id, a part of the personality that wants things and would do anything to get them. The Id is motivated by pure dire but needs the ego in order to negotiate to get things it wants.

As I sat there waiting for the Holy Spirit and as Ben and Wil talked with the oldest daughter, I began to hear the Lord tell me to wait for the witch girl to leave then bless the home and place scripture in the cracks outside. At first I thought it was odd but then thought I shouldn't disobey the Lord. And so I waited to see if the youngest was going to leave. After a while I didn't think she would but she came down from the upstairs with a small purse and began heading for the front door. Her oldest sister quickly asked her where she was going. The young witch mentioned that she was leaving with her boyfriend. The oldest was quick to inform her of their mother's wishes but the youngest ignored her and left anyway. I was a little amazed that she left when the small still voice of the Lord told me what would happen. After the young witch left I informed Ben, Wil and the eldest daughter of what I wanted to do. They agreed and left to go outside.

I was alone in the house. I got out my bag of tricks as I called it and retrieved my anointing oil, holy water, and prayer book. It was quiet in the house and I had pictures in my mind of what may happen. I had never blessed a home or performed an exorcism before and was solely going off what the Holy Spirit and my mentors told me. My instant thought was that when I would start reading from the prayer book that doors would slam shut, furniture would turn over and odd noises would echo in the house. As I began to read with a knotted throat nothing was happening. I went into the basement, blessed it and nothing happened. I went upstairs into all the rooms and nothing happened. Everywhere I went to anoint with oil and throw holy water, saying the prayer, nothing was happening. I assumed that since nothing was happening that the spirits must have left with the witch. I almost stopped praying at times, thinking that I had to face the demons to cast them out, but each time I stopped could hear the Lord tell me "Continue and don't stop."

I finished blessing the inside of the house and proceeded to the outside. Ben, Wil and the eldest daughter moved back into the house as we traded positions. I had a little pocket size Bible with me and I was surprised to hear the Lord tell me to rip pages out of it and place them in the cracks of the home and say a prayer over the paper. So I did and walked around the house looking for cracks; ripping pages out of the little Bible and placing them in the cracks, saying a prayer for protection over each one. When I was done I made my way to the front door and went inside. I informed Ben that I was leaving and asked if he needed a ride. Wil spoke up and said that he could take him home. He then left to go out to his car and retrieved his paints. Wil was a painter on the side making extra money for his family. The mother had asked him before I visited to paint the girl's room white when I got done blessing the home. I left but not without requesting for Ben and Wil to update me on the condition of the case. They agreed and I left for the long trek north to Central Michigan.

A week later I didn't hear anything back from Ben or Wil so I decided to call them to find out how things were going in the home I blessed. Wil answered his phone in the deep rapper tone he had. I asked how things were going with the young girl. He replied in excitement and began to explain the details for me. Wil mentioned that when the young witch came home she completely changed when she entered the door. She went to church that Sunday and threw up when she entered the sanctuary. The girl threw up again during service, then a third time after service. I quickly recalled how Ben and Wil discerned that she had three demons. Wil even claimed to have seen one of them appear behind her in the kitchen while I was there. A shadow figure of some kind popped its head up from behind her shoulder. Apparently the young witch had a change of heart over her friends as well and left them behind. The old witch herself who tried to convert her heard what happen to the fourteen year old and had a change of heart as well and converted to Christianity.

When our conversation ended I gave all glory to God and thanked him for being my mentor in the case and for using me as his tool for helping deliver this family from occult darkness. My first deliverance allowed me to realize that the best way to perform deliverance was to go by the guidance of the Holy Spirit; listen and obey. We are not able to see the supernatural so I realized how much better it is to put our pride behind and follow the Spirit of God who is able to see everything. I didn't know it then but my first work of deliverance was called ekballism. With a word and guidance of the Holy Spirit I cast the demons out of several lives, not just one. That event became the first in a long domino chain, setting the motion for a revival in a church as well. You see the church that the girl vomited in saw firsthand that there is in fact a darkness that is attacking humanity. What I learnt from that case was that a demonic case is always used for the glory of God. Where there is a demonic case or a horrific haunting started by the Devil, God will always turn it around for good in His favor. It is the job of the ekballist to keep that in mind; follow the leading of God, even if the case doesn't work out, because in some fashion God has used that case for His glory.

We always hear the phrase, *"God acts in mysterious ways"* and that is so true in deliverance ministry. The problem with a lot of ministers who perform deliverance believe that the end is where the demon is cast out. That is not the case. The end is where God is glorified in whatever way He chooses to be glorified. Win or lose, the ekballist will always see where God is glorified and his job is to make sure people see it. That is where the victory is. One person is always being affected by the devil in a case but in the end many are converted and God always wins. For it is God's concern for mankind not to be caught up in this life, but the next, and that we are saved to get there.

tHE EARLY YEARS

My life was filled with supernatural events since I was a baby. My mother told me that when she brought me home from the hospital after I was born she was rocking me in front of the picture window and saw a ball of light shoot across the top of the pines. Our little child minds never seem to want to record anything when we are just babies. I've known a lot of people who asked their parents what happened the day they were born. For me that was the event that stuck out the most in my life when I thought about the day I first came home. I always thought how interesting it was to know that and to have the person I most admired, my mother, recalling it for me. I can honestly say that event was the first paranormal activity I was around even though I don't remember it.

Growing up I've always had a weird saying running through my head. My family knew about God but was secular, never teaching my brother and I anything about Him. My mother's old Bible with a zipper on it always interested me but that was about it. I never read the Bible but what spooked me and allowed me to become interested in Jesus Christ was when my mother purchased Christian name cards for my brother and I. The cards gave our names meaning and a verse for each one. Mine said, *"Latin origin meaning 'Guardian', God's trustee."* I recall thinking how interesting that was; then I saw the verse and my mouth dropped when I read it. There before me was the saying that ran through my head from when I was a baby. It read, *"The Lord is my shepherd I shall not want, Psalm 23:1"* I remember asking my mom how to use a Bible and look up verses. When I finally found it I began to cry and couldn't believe what I just experienced. To this day Psalm 23:1 has always defined my personal ministry.

However, the first time I encountered what I thought was a ghost was something else. When my brother and I were young our parents would take turns visiting one of our grandparent's home once a week. This time it was my mother's parents we were going to visit and I was excited. Most of the time aunts and uncles were there on the farm and would bring my cousins with them. My cousins and I would play out in the barn or the tractor shed, sometimes we would pretend we were racing our uncle's cars he was always trying to fix up. We all thought my uncle who stayed on the farm to help my grandparents was cool. We used to watch him in the garage working on old cars but we would get too close and he would yell at us to step back. I look back now and envy him because he had a 1970 Pontiac GTO. When I got older he bought a LeManes at a police auction but had to hide it for a while because he found out that the previous owner had left prison and was looking for his car.

When my father informed us that we were visiting the farm I was excited and hopeful to see my cousins. I recall riding in the back seat on the way there with my brother. I could almost remap the route in my child head on what roads to take to get to the old farm. The old abandoned country school on the corner that my mother went to when she was young was still there. The old school was an anchor in my memory to signal when we would arrive near the farm and turn down the dirt road. We would arrive and pull in to see my great-grandfather's old home sitting abandoned, while next door was the new house where my mother grew up. My grandfather was going to inherit the farm so he built a house close to his father's to help on the farm. He and my grandmother had four boys and two girls who helped their parents and grandparents work on the farm. My mother always told me how she would play with the chickens and milk the cows. To the north my father grew up on a separate farm and was how my parents met over time. His parents later sold their farm and moved to the city.

Anyone who ever visited my grandparents' farm always walked in the back door and went through the kitchen. My grandmother always seemed to be in the kitchen making some sort of food for the large family of farmers. When the farmers came back from the fields she had breakfast, lunch and dinner ready. We'd usually laugh that my grandfather and uncles would eat huge portions while my grandmother would just eat a salad. Times were simpler then and money wasn't so tight. There always seemed to be food on the table all day every day. There was so much food that it would be at the edge of the table. If you pushed on a bowl to hard you'd be moving everything on the table forcing someone's plate to move. You'd get a mouth full from them and they'd push everything back. I only recall one time when something fell on the floor and everyone paused and the greatest generation, my grandparents, began to lecture everyone.

I entered the kitchen with my parents and greeted my grandmother. We always had to take our shoes off or risk being yelled at. I walked in and was disappointed that I didn't see any of my cousins there. As a child I quickly knew that I was going to be bored so I got out the toy box that grandma saved for us grandkids. I was in kindergarten or first grade at the time and while I played with the toys I didn't like to be bothered. However, my grandfather always asked how we were doing. He was old school through and through but an emotional man. Looking back I can see how the things he did, that may have seemed rude or offensive, were actually acts of love. As a joke he would always offer us grandkids a pinch of chewing tobacco. No one would take any of course but one time I tried just to see what he would do. As my hand moved in he moved the can of Copenhagen back away from me and told me how he better not let me have a pinch or else my mom would yell at him. When we would get older and have girlfriends he would always ask us grandsons if we had a girlfriend. If we answered yes he'd get excited and ask us if they were black or white. My brother jokingly replied black one time and my grandfather became excited more and replied how my brother had to be careful because the black would rub off. No matter whom you were if you bent over to pick something up he would pinch your rear and if you stood up and looked at him he would mention how he was just helping you. He was a practical joker up until the day he passed away.

Over the course of the night I became bored and wanted to leave. I asked my parents if we could and they replied in a half hour, which in their good bye terms meant an hour. I knew that once they got started with their good byes it would be at least two hours before we'd be in the car. I wanted to leave to go home and sleep so I walked to the door in the kitchen, leaving everyone in the living room behind.

I put my shoes on and got back up and walked to the kitchen door. To the left was another door that led upstairs. The door was always closed for some odd reason. I just assumed that they didn't want anyone going up there, but when I asked about it later my grandmother informed me that the ceiling was weak. Just as I touched the door and wrapped my tiny hands around the knob I felt a cold sensation and started to hear a creaking sound. I instantly became paralyzed with fear as the door leading to the upstairs beside me slowly crept open. I mustered any strength I had to turn my head and just as I did I viewed the door fully opening. I began to hear whispering and I tried to run away but I couldn't. My heart was beating fast and the door knob felt like a magnet on my hand. As much as I tried to pull my hand free I couldn't, then the door slowly began to close and latched shut. As I heard the click the fear that came over me began to go away and I was able to slowly pull my hand off the door knob. I backed away slowly from the door until I was in the middle of the kitchen, turned and fast walked back to my parents. I stood in the living room crying and mentioned to my elders how I saw a ghost. I didn't actually see the ghost, I had only experienced it being near me and whispering. They didn't know what to think and my parents told me it wasn't a ghost but I knew what I experienced wasn't normal but rather abnormal for everyday living. I wanted to go but I didn't want to walk by the door so I asked to go out the front door instead. My father picked me up crying and we left through the back door, passing that door that lead upstairs and out to the car.

As I grew up I learned from my mother and uncles that my great-grandfather on my grandma's side passed away in that house. But I also learnt that grandma used to use the Ouija board to help find objects that were lost on the farm. As time went by growing up through elementary school and on to middle school I had a hard time trying to walk passed that door when walking in through the kitchen to visit my grandparents. My cousins thought that my story of what I experienced was funny and used to hide behind the door and wait for me to walk in and scare me. Over time I finally overcame the fear I had when walking past that door but I'd never forget it; it was my first experience with an evil spirit.

I know what you are saying right now, "It sounds like a ghost." Well, it does but the thing is you weren't there. When I stood there frozen with my hand locked to the door knob, I felt the sensation that my life was in danger. I had a vision of the spirit in that moment also. It was a vision of child-like person with oily hair and deep black eyes sunken in their skull. It was smiling at me also as if it were sinister and trying to scare me on purpose. It could have done anything to me at that moment. I even felt the sensation like it wanted to pull me onto the stair case and up the stairs, kidnap me and torment me. It was as if the spirit was telling me, "I can take you and your parents wouldn't even know you were gone because they would think you are playing."

I'll never forget that moment in my life. It stands in the back of my mind like a cold dark shiver, a chill that runs up your spine.

ENTERING THE OCCULT

Throughout my youth I had a struggle over whether or not there was a God. The saying that went through my head and the Christian name cards always stuck in my mind. It was a huge question mark in my life that caused me to question my existence. I couldn't believe how shocking it was. What was it that God wanted me to do? What is it that he put me on this earth for? What was my purpose? I had tons of questions that weren't getting answered. To me it was obvious that I was meant to do something but I couldn't figure out what. In my youth I became obsessed with knowing what Psalm 23:1 meant. *"The Lord is my Shepherd, I shall not want."* It bugged me. At first the verse sounded like I didn't want the Lord as my shepherd. Why did that happen? I asked myself. Over and over I kept thinking of that verse through elementary school. I recall one moment in first grade looking out the huge windows in the classroom from my desk, watching it rain. The water acted like a waterfall against the glass. There weren't any gutters on the edges of that old school so when it rained you could see the water flowing down the big windows. Recess was canceled due to flash flooding. I intently thought of that verse and its meaning.

In second grade I thought of that verse as if my conscience was on fire. By third grade I recalled the verse still and received my first pattle because I was pushed by friends to misbehave in class. I was a good kid and never really got into trouble. I didn't understand why there was war or why people fought. In some ways I understood God and His view of the world. I thought war, hatred, adultery and all were stupid and didn't understand why adults did them. Times seemed to be simpler then. However, I started to understand why adults do the things they do when I got into high school. I seemed to fit in with all kinds of crowds because I didn't want to be prejudice toward anyone. I played sports mainly football and baseball. My grandfather on my father's side showed me how to hit. He would always sit and watch the Detroit Tigers in his house and when you blocked the television he'd let you know that you had to move. He studied how the professionals hit the ball and showed me. I tried it in games, asking the Lord to give me a clean hit each time. I was known in school as a designated hitter and would get doubles and triples.

In my high school years I finally made a decision on what to do with God in my life. I decided to be an atheist and put that silly verse behind me. I'd look at my hand at times and see the ape but the feet comparison was confusing. However, silly evolution was I decided to accept it as fact. In some ways it felt right to me. I didn't feel any more pressure but at times I would hear my conscience bug me and tell me that I was making the wrong decision. I wanted to fit in, get with the girls and be cool. The only reason why I became an atheist was the same reason why atheist's today are the way they are. I knew that if there was a God that I wouldn't be able to do the things I wanted to do; namely to sin with pleasure and be independent. It felt good to be an atheist and not have a care. In some ways I grasped the animal instinct and held on.

I recall a dream I had one night when I was a freshman; but really it was more of a vision. I saw myself standing in town walking up the steps of a church wearing the whole priestly garb, suit collar and all. It was as if God was giving me a vision of my future at the time. I dismissed the vision and put it behind me. I didn't want to be a priest because I wanted to get married and have a family. At the time I didn't understand the Christian denominations and thought that all priests didn't get married. I wanted to be an artist and create some wild art and get famous. My dream was to live off my artwork selling paintings for hundreds and thousands of dollars. It was a wild dream but I took art classes in high school and by the time I became a senior I could take an independent study course with the art teacher who took me under her wing. I had to walk every morning from the high school to the junior high but it was worth it. I felt like I was in college from the details my brother described at the time. He told me how he had to walk or bike to class from building to building and back to his dorm room. I couldn't wait to go to college and learn more on art and design.

After the art classes I was a teacher's aide for the gym teacher at the junior high, helping to grade papers and setting up events for him. Then at noon I had to walk back to the high school to finish up my day. During the walks to and from the junior high I made new friends who were involved in the occult. They didn't talk much about it but seemed to leave me out of conversations, talking about various things. Finally I spoke up one day in the autumn when they were talking about Halloween stuff. I asked them what they do and they told me they play with tarot cards and have tried to cast spells. I laughed at first and thought it was silly. I didn't believe them due to my decision of being an atheist but something struck, shocked me rather when they told me stories of one of my good friends who was a couple of grades ahead of me. Joe had already graduated and lived alone east of town. Some of them would visit him and he'd teach some things on occult uses. I knew Joe through mutual friends and grew to like him. I was shocked to hear stories of how Joe's place was haunted and how he wanted to get out of the occult but felt bound to it. When I was a junior in high school I remember a friend named Jon telling me how Joe invited him over to his place and gave him all his occult material to burn. Jon had asked him about the book of the dead he had, the necronomicon as they called it, Joe went and retrieved it and threw it on the table. Joe pointed at it and said to Jon, "Take that thing back and burn it also." As the story goes Joe said that the book began to levitate. Of course I didn't believe it when Jon told me because I knew the book was a work of fiction but thought it was an interesting story he told; that was all. The necronomicon is a fictional book that a horror author named H.P. Lovecraft made up, although as I later got into demonology I discovered that Lovecraft's references in the necronomicon are no different than how the way the Bible references the Book of Enoch and many other non-canonical books left out of the Bible. When I was young I could see how the necronomicon was fictional but later understood how demons were able to influence through literature. As long as someone created something through wicked or evil means with influences through the flesh, the demonic could use it as a channel by which to gain control. But still I craved a connection of some kind to the supernatural even though I believed it was a work of fiction. I realized that maybe I wasn't an atheist but maybe an agnostic due to my mysterious encounter when I was young. I began to think that maybe the occult was the way to go to find answers.

I knew Joe and thought I should ask him myself of what was going on with him. We had a mutual friend name Ray who drove me over to Joe's one day to hang out. I bugged Joe about his occult usage and he didn't want to talk about it. Ray told me in front of Joe what Joe would do and some wild stories about spirits he encountered. They both told me the time when Ted spent the night at Joe's and they were woken by three very loud bangs on the side of the house. Both Ray and Joe ran outside to see who it was, thinking it was the neighbor kids. No one was around. They went back inside and sat back down trying to figure out who it could have been when there were three very loud bangs on the side of the house again. Again they ran outside as soon as it happened and still no one was around. Their stories had brought me back to my first experience on the farm. I told them what happened to me when I was a child on the farm and Joe's eye brow rose. He asked me if anyone had a Ouija board in that house and I told him how my grandmother would use one to help her find things on the farm that were lost. In old times it was tradition for farmers to use occult items to gain insight about things. Some would break a wish-bone size branch off a tree and go looking for water to make a well. Others would place octograms or hexagrams on the sides of their barns to ward off misfortune, evil spirits and disease. Still to this day some farmers will swear by the farmer's almanac to know the coming year's weather.

Joe began to shake his head and informed me that what I experienced was an evil spirit from that board. Joe also told me how he had one and used it to tell him his future and find out about hidden things. That did it for me. I wanted in and wanted to use the occult. I wanted Joe to be my mentor on how to use the occult. The thought of being able to use magick, spells and knowing my future intrigue me. I wanted power, real power and riches but it all fell apart when Joe informed me that he wouldn't teach me anything. He was done with the occult and wanted out. He wanted to move on with his life and get rid of whatever spirit was following him. Joe looked at me and gave me a warning to stay away from the occult.

THE FORTUNE

I decided not to listen to Joe and went to a book store, and
purchased tarot cards and a few spell books. I remember feeling almost
sick when I bought them and having to push my conscience to the side
in order to make the purchase. I didn't know how to use them but
knew that Ray had seen how Joe laid them out before. He invited me
out to his house and I showed him the cards, he was instantly shocked
that I didn't take Joe's warning seriously. I asked Ray to tell me how
Joe used them but he only knew how he laid them out but didn't know
what the layout meant. He started from the bottom laying them down,
one after the other until he finished. What I saw were two cards over
top each other in a plus sign then four cards laid out in four directions.
Off to the side were four more cards. I asked what it meant. Ray didn't
know and informed me that he only saw how Joe laid them out.
Suddenly Joe walked in Ray's bedroom and saw us with tarot cards
and quickly walked out. We were surprised that Joe drove over to pay
Ray a visit. Ray's mom had allowed Joe in the house and in Ray's
room. Ray quickly grabbed Joe and brought him back in the room but
he wasn't willing to be near the cards. I asked Joe how to use the cards
but he refused to show me. I kept asking until he caved and began to
point at each section in the tarot lay out. He informed us of how the
cards laid out like a cross told your past. The outlaying cards were the
present and the cards off to the side were the future. However, the
person whose fortune was being told had to either shuffle the deck or

cut the cards. Joe grabbed the cards and began shuffling them. His eyes closed as he shuffled and he mentioned how the cards felt good. "These are good cards." He said, and I stood there in wonder over what that meant. I asked him if he could tell me my fortune. He agreed but it would be the last fortune he would tell.

Joe handed me the tarot cards and asked me to shuffle them. I did, giving them a good shuffle and handed them back to him. He laid the cards out on Ray's bed as we watched. When Joe was done he looked over the cards and seemed to be excited. He looked at me and informed me that I would have three true loves and with the fourth one I would rush in like a knight. Ray was wowed over the fortune but Joe didn't go there. Joe told me that this fortune was already in the works and said that whatever I was doing now would make me wealthy in the future. I instantly thought of my artwork. I was excited to believe that my artwork would be so successful that it would make me wealthy. Joe and Ray were excited for me and they themselves thought it would be my artwork. I also thought of other things that I was doing that could make me wealthy at the time but wasn't sure. "It actually could be anything", Joe told me and informed me that it could be right under my nose and I wouldn't even know until it happened. I asked him again about the three true loves and he gave me a warning that these true loves would be so strong that I would nearly kill myself each time. I didn't believe it but I recall going home looking forward to meeting my first true love. I knew that if I fell in love and felt it was true that I would know the fortune was true. I recall Joe pointing at the lover's and the knight of swords cards and describing how my fourth true love would be the one I would marry and be wealthy with.

It's everyone's wish to be wealthy in their life. The thought of being financially secure when the economy goes bad and you're standing out on top is a dream that everyone wants. To win the lottery and getting handed a check for millions of dollars. Inventing and getting commission checks from a major industry when your invention becomes famous. These and more are some of the dreams that people have. My dream at the time of hearing my fortune was that my artwork would become famous. I truly believed it would be that craft that would make me tons of money, Joe and Ray believed it also. I was one of two popular artists in school. I would draw in class and show the other kids who thought my work was cool.

As I went on through my life with this fortune in the back of my mind it was as if the devil was playing cruel jokes on me. Pieces of the fortune did come true and come to past, such as my four true loves. The first true love made me think that the wealth part of the fortune jumped the gun. I was playing the monopoly game from McDonald's for the first time. McDonald's placed game pieces in the Sunday newspaper and when I claimed the game pieces I instantly got boardwalk. I placed it on the board and decided to play. I got a stroke of luck and felt fortune was on its way. Others who knew I had the game piece told me that it would be impossible to receive park place. Over time and many value meals later I decided to quit playing and threw the board away in the trash. A few days later I was driving through a town and ordered at McDonald's, checked the game pieces and got park place. I drove home quickly and began looking through the trash but only to learn that the trash was already taken out. You're probably reading this thinking how much of a fool I was to throw away the boardwalk game piece. Actually at the time I thought myself a fool but when I look back at it now I realize that it this was actually a good event in my life. You see the girl I was with at the time whom I believed was my first true love actually torn my heart out. I fell head over heels in love for her and she was one of the worst decisions I ever made. If I would have kept playing the game and won the million dollars I would have been rich. However, I would have also had been an unwise teenage kid who would have dropped out of school, married this girl, and together we would have spent all the money on stupid things. Then we would have gotten divorced and if we would have had any kids they would have gone with her because of the state's laws favoring the mother over the father. I would have been miserable but when I jokingly tell this story to new friends I laugh and say that I can honestly say I threw away a million dollars for true happiness. I like to think that it was God looking out for me when I was a foolish kid making wrong decisions. I look back at that event and am so glad that I threw it away. As I got older and wiser I began to believe the logic that a person needs to be wise in order to have money. Today I know a couple of rich people. They are wise with their money and don't spend it wildly like I would have when I was a teen. What I learned from that experience is that riches don't bring happiness; true joy comes from knowing the Lord.

I met a girl in college who liked poetry. She drew my interest and we began dating. I would spend nights at her house near the college for days; and interestingly her house was haunted. It was a minor haunt with the ghost only wanting some attention at times. I didn't believe her at first but when she turned a light on in a room and informed me that that the ghost liked to turn it off at midnight, and it did, I became a believer. Sometimes the ghost would shake the plates near the sink but that was all it would do. Whether or not it was actually haunted remains a mystery. The banging of the plates could have actually had been a mouse, and the light going off at midnight may have been some type of surge or something from the electrical company that went on every night. But the thing was, the dishes would raddle hard as if someone were in the kitchen; and the thing that got me were the times waking up in the morning to find all the cupboard doors open.

This girl wasn't my second true love but she did do something interesting. Later in our relationship I was thinking about breaking up with her. I started to like someone else who would become my second true love. The interesting thing this girl did was visit a psychic/fortune teller who told her our fortune as a couple. At this time in my life it was a year or two after my first encounter with a demon during the witching hour that nearly took my life. So I was a little upset that she had done such a thing because at that moment in my life I knew the dangers of the occult.

She informed me everything the psychic said and did with the tarot. The psychic informed her that she could read her fine but when she tried to read me it was as if someone had put a brick wall up. I was a little shocked and it made me wonder if God was interfering again in my life, protecting me. But the really interesting thing was that the fortune teller informed her that we would break up soon. My mouth dropped and I didn't know what to say. She was worried that we were going to break up and I sat her down and talked with her. I felt bad but I told her what had been on my mind. She was shocked and agreed to the break up. She was so hurt that while we were attending the same college she left. I never saw her again. After that relationship I swore I would never metal with divination again. It is one thing to get your fortune told, but while the evil spirits will tell you what will happen in your life, you have to give them something in return. That is the real danger, and generally we don't tell them what we will give them so they assume it is our lives. People who get their fortunes told to them by fortune tellers receive a piece of an evil spirit and don't realize it. In the book of Acts Paul cast out a demon from a fortune teller who was making men who owned her an income. She was free from the spirit of divination but the men were angry that they lost their one source of money. The fortune teller and the person who receives the fortune don't feel the spirit transfer, but believe me it is there. If you have ever received a fortune, renounce it and put it at the foot of the cross.

My second true love was a doll. I was a little wiser at this time and could see myself marrying her, starting a family when I graduated from college and found a good job to start my career. I was with her for most of my college years and she saw me graduate. We had a romance. We were two lovers who would skip class and travel out to places and spend time away from the worries of the world. After class I would hurry to the library where she worked and watched her from a far until she was able to get out.

The first time I met her was when I went to the library with friends. She was there working and I was stunned by her beauty. I wanted to eagerly meet her so I quickly got on the computer nearest to the librarian counter and tried hard to find out where she was on the internet. I asked one of my friends to walk behind her to see where she was online. He came back and showed me. I found her handle in a chatroom and began talking to her until I told her that I was in the same college and library as her. She quickly stood up and looked around and I mentioned her actions to her in the chatroom. I finally mentioned to her what I was wearing and she quickly spotted me. I knew I broke the difficult ice with her when she saw me and smiled. She got up and walked over, greeting me. I asked for her phone number and we began to date.

The problem with me was that in the back of my mind I still wanted my fortune to come true. I was picky and wanted to know who the last two women that were to come would be. I broke up with her twice but the last time I tried to get her back she wouldn't have me. It was over. She was perfect in every way but my need for the college experience and women brought out the fool in me again. I drank with my college friends to cut the pain until I finally decided to move on.

My third true love I met while I was working in retail. When I dated her I made other men at work jealous. I had a knack with the girls. If I saw a girl I wanted to date I would watch them and study them, see what they liked and developed a rapport with them. When I felt the right moment arrived I would attack like a lion and ask the question that men in their twenties dreaded to ask single women; "Would you like to go out sometime?"

She had a daughter whom at times I thought of as my own. We were with each other for a while but as time went by I realized that I hit a new low by dating her. She would pawn her daughter off on others and take off. At times she would do this to my parents and it would seem like for days she wouldn't see her daughter. Toward the end I found out she was cheating on me, being gone for days on end until finally I called the relationship off. She was angry to say the least but it was one of the hardest things I did. I feel in love with her but it seemed like she put up a front with me, wanting me to see someone else rather than the real person she was. Breaking up was hard for me. I asked God for guidance and realized that I needed to find myself a woman with good family values, wise, a family woman, and someone who would love me for who I am and would never leave me. I decided I wanted a Christian girl. A woman who at least believed in God and could look deep inside of me to get me straightened out. I now knew what I wanted and I found her at the same retail store. My ex-girlfriend had quit and moved away but by the time she found out who I was dating next she became jealous. I never heard from her again.

One day I had walked over to the deli in the store to order lunch when I saw a new girl in the bakery. I was curious and walked over past the bakery and caught a glimpse of her. She had beautiful long blonde hair and a smile that caught my eye. I was instantly curious as to who she was. Over time I would meet her and finally decide to ask her on a date. I had a lot of butterflies in my stomach and she met me at the bakery counter. I asked her out and she told me how she would like to go out on a date with me but she had a boyfriend. I bid her good bye and walked away with my confidence shot. I always felt a bit of disgust with myself when I was turned down by a woman. From what my co-workers told me about her, this woman sounded like the woman of my dreams. She was adorable, uplifting, confident and loved people. A part of me mysteriously believed that she was the one. But I didn't believe it. I wasn't even thinking about the fortune that Jon gave me, I just thought of being happy and finding the right woman for me. At this time I had put that silly fortune behind me.

After a short period of time her and her boyfriend had broken up. Like the lion I was I saw an opportunity and I asked her out again and she agreed. I wanted our first date to be special so I told her to dress up because I was going to take her to see an orchestra at a local college in the fall. When we got there we laughed because we were the only ones who were dressed up while others were wearing plain clothes. We watched as the musicians played the classics from Beethoven to Mozart and Pachelbel. Our second date we both read to each other our poetry that we wrote over the years.

We were comfortable with each other and could tell each other anything. We fell in love and in a couple of years in June we were married at the sound of bagpipes in a Methodist church. I got a great job, we built a home and we were happy. Prior to the building of our new home my father's dad, my grandfather passed away.

We never made tons of money or became wealthy. We were actually lower middle class but we were content with what we had. We sometimes wished we had enough money to feel secure but still we were happy. Over time we had tons of friends and brought many people to Christ through our ministry work together. That to me was true wealth. Jesus said to give all you have and store up treasures in Heaven. Together we were giving to our ministry all that we had, training people for the work of evangelism and bringing people to the cross of Christ. To me we had stored up treasures in Heaven and that was worth more than any wealth made by man.

THE SORCERER

As I read and studied books on the occult I made a decision of what direction to go with in the occult. I decided to be a sorcerer. I felt that it was the most powerful position in the occult and so I studied on how to move objects, summon spirits to do things for me and to influence people into doing things I wanted them to do. I wanted to add my own twist to sorcery by adding psi power and the abilities of psychics. I was interested in mind over matter and wanted to perfect it. It was also about this time that I started playing Dungeons & Dragons with friends. The game influenced me to get into spell casting and dabble even further into the occult. I never understood the rumors that the game would drive people to possession and thought it was nonsense. I look back at that now and think of how wrong I was. The game doesn't do anything whatsoever. It is so well designed that it takes a person away from their worries, pain and suffering, opening their imagination. Each person has their own character in role-playing and by the throw of the dice a person who designs each mission, the Dungeon Master, tells you what is happening. Like I said, you can play the game all you want and walk away from it not becoming possessed. All the game acts like is an introduction to the occult; much like marijuana introduces people to other drugs. The game can get a person interested in wanting to learn about spell casting outside of the game in the real world. Some people who play the game put real spells in it and cast them while playing. That is where the real danger of the game is.

Every noon hour at school my friends and I would meet in a classroom and role-play. I started out with a magic-user and killed him off by fighting with a god over a wand of lightning on accident and ended up with a thief. Many people at school thought that there was just one D&D group but the truth is there was actually two. Some of us went between the groups and when the game was advanced enough each side was thinking about starting a war.

Many other kids at school wanted in on the game but we kept it secret and away from the eyes of the other kids. However, the other group began to play in the middle of class during free times. This drove the original group to want to start a war. With their Dungeon Master's the two groups were going through time and quickly advancing in levels to obtain power. It was like a cold war in D&D. Each side was threatening to go to war and secretly obtaining weapons of war and mass armies. It was at this time when God was slowly coming back into my life. I had the most powerful cleric out of both of the groups and I made him a Christian. His god was thee God and for a small period of time I held back from my studies as a sorcerer. However, it didn't last long. I finally pulled myself away from the D&D group and continued studying. My main focus was telekinesis, the ability to move objects. I got to the point that I was able to move water while it was dripping out of a faucet. I could bend the small stream of water left or right just by thinking about it. Other things began to happen also. I would worry about money and for some time money would show up either in my pocket or on my dresser at home. I asked my parents if they gave me any money and they replied that they didn't. I later learned that sorcerers didn't have to worry about working and obtaining money because as much as they thought about it the money would show up for them.

I became a believer in the supernatural and felt that my skills were being successful but still needed a lot of improvement. I was curious of Satanism but I would never touch the stuff. I heard rumors of covens in neighboring towns and how they would seek out children for their rituals. Those were just rumors of course. All I wanted was the power to control my surroundings. As much as I would practice telekinesis to make it work I was never successful at it. However, the small things that did happen caused me to be a believer that there was a world out there that was unseen just as that spirit on the farm. A part of me did worry of *what if* an evil spirit was following me or *what if* I had invoked one by mistake? After all Joe mentioned that he was trying to get rid of something that was following him. I didn't know the first thing on how to remove it or make it go away. I couldn't even tell if something was in me. But in the back of my mind I kept getting the feeling like I was being watched.

tHE wiTcHinq HOUR

My first encounter with a demon was in the fall of 1993, when two of my friends and I were invited to a party in a small Mid-Michigan town. Ray and Nicolas had picked me up and drove me to the party where many of the kids that were there I'd never met before, being locals from a neighboring school. The only kids I knew were Nicolas, Ray and Ray's sister Ruth. Ruth was living in the house with a friend at the time and they decided to host the party. A lot of the kids that were there were involved in some way in the occult but others were there just to party.

As the night went on some of the guys grabbed the phone and began dialing numbers from the phone book anonymously. They pretended to be local radio disc jockeys, telling people that answered that if they could scream loud enough over the phone they could win free money. Little did the people on the other end of the phone know that it was all a prank and there was no free money. However, the comedians got many people to scream over the phone and many party goers laughed.

I never drank much in my youth. I tried my best to not drink at all; but to fit in I decided to drink one or two beers at parties that I attended. Little did some of my friends know I actually kept the same beer most of the night and acted like I was getting more. It wasn't until my college years that I fully decided to drink, and it wasn't until I met the woman who would later be my wife that I wised up and stopped all together. I had lost a good friend of mine to alcohol, a cousin, and a fellow high school football team mate to the stuff and I wasn't about to live an addictive life style to alcohol.

As the night dragged on many of the kids got bored and many began to sober up. Some people even left the party and the atmosphere began to settle down after the phone pranks. It wasn't until Ruth got out her new Ouija™ board that the atmosphere really started to calm down and everyone was acting normal. Another girl got out another Ouija™ board and they both began to call upon spirits. A state of quiet began to fill the house as Ruth and her friend moved the planchette on the boards with each question being asked. At first it seemed nothing worked but then by some unseen hands the planchette seemed to move across the board with ease. Some of the kids asked funny questions getting a laugh out of the others, but after the laughs died down all eyes were on the boards. The room was dark and lit by a single lamp in the living area. It had seemed that the answers were coming across very slow as the planchette spelled out words, so I tried to see if I could channel whatever it was that was trying to communicate through the board. I wanted to play a trick on Ruth and know what her board was trying to say before she could spell out the words.

Over a short period of time my efforts to read the boards didn't work as each question was being asked. Ruth had even told me to be quiet. Others were wondering what I was trying to do. Finally it happened. I began to foresee what the board was going to say before Ruth and her friend could spell out the words with the planchette. The whole house became eerie. If a drop of water had fallen from a faucet I think it would have went to the ceiling instead of hitting the sink. The atmosphere felt misty and heavy at the same time. I began saying the answers to the questions people had with complete accuracy to her board. Frightened, Ruth looked up at me and told me that I was scaring her. After a few more answers to questions, I blacked out. It was like going through a time warp. At one moment I was in the living room sitting Indian style watching Ruth and her friend play with the boards. When I came to, I discovered myself on the porch with the crowd over me, crying. It was a scene from the movie Jumper. One moment I was in the living room and in a split second I was on the porch with no knowledge on how I got there. On both of my arms were two big guys trying to hold me down. I recall asking how I got out on the porch. One of the guys holding me down stared into my eyes and told the party goers he thought I had returned. I had no memory of how I got onto the porch. I looked up at Ruth and witnessed her reading scripture from a Bible in her hands. Then I blacked out again.

The second time I came to I was on the couch and overheard people yelling in terror. Some of the girls were crying and afraid that I was going to die. I was weak and could hardly move. One man said that I was so cold to the touch that they ran and got blankets to cover me. Another man said that I looked very pale. My vision became blurry then I passed out and fell asleep.

I had felt like I was levitating in air going higher and higher. As I could make out what was happening my vision came back and I saw a man carry me upstairs to a room and lay me on a bed. At this point I felt that I was hit by a truck and very tired. I could see light come into the room and looked over the bed board to see a square window. When I looked through it I could see a full moon. I starred at it for a while and asked God what happened to me. For the first time in my occult life I called out to God. I remember seeing the craters on the moon and tried counting each one. It was beautiful in something dark as the night sky. The moon reflected the light from the sun. Knowing that the light coming from the moon was actually reflected from the unseen sun, that moment felt like God was separated from me. I felt as dirty as the moon but then it hit me, all the knowledge and experience I obtained could be used to help others. I could reflect God's light off my dirty sinful existence onto others; if God would have me. All I wanted to do was go home at that point to my parents and my bed, forgetting about what ever embarrassment I may take in the morning; then I fell asleep.

Several times during the night I was woken up by my friends asking me how I was doing. I kept asking them what happened but they always stated that they also wanted to know.

Finally my friends woke me up early in the morning and while the party goers were asleep, they took me out of the house and drove me home. We never talked much but when we did I asked what happened. Nicolas was in disagreement, while Ray was confused and told me that he would tell me later when he could make sense of everything. Ray would have probably understood more of what happened due to his mild involvement in the occult. Nicolas and I talked a few times later but he never wanted to discuss what happened. I never saw him again.

Two days later I met up with Ray and begged him to tell me what had happened. He looked at me funny. "You honestly don't know?" Ray said staring at me.

"No, I don't." I replied, telling him what I did remember up to the Ouija™ board session then Ray explained what happened after.

"Many people witnessed a black mass come over you, then you started making these eerie sounds and an inhuman voice came out of you. You stood up and started babbling some strange language. A man walked over to you and told you to shut up, so you picked him up and threw him on the coffee table, breaking it. I walked up to you and saw your face and eyes, how red they were and I knew it wasn't you. I told you to stop; you pushed me and ran for the kitchen door. I grabbed some guys and we tackled you and that was how you found yourself on the porch."

This is the only thing I can recall from that night through an eye witness. Other than his testimony there was no way I could have known what happened. Many of the party goers never stepped forward to tell their account of the events that night. Some say the experience was so terrifying that no one wanted to talk about it.

Ray and I remained friends for a few more years then lost contact. Later we met up a few times and each time I would ask a little more of what happen. He never wanted to talk about it.

The experience lasted in my spirit like a scar on skin. The flesh gets cut and if it doesn't receive stitches it bumps up and forms a brighter line or mark on the skin revealing a scar. The scar doesn't go away and acts as a reminder of how it got there.

AFTER THE ATTACK

After my attack by a dark entity my faith in God was cemented. I knew beyond a shadow of a doubt that there was a God after what I experienced. However, I was traumatized by the whole thing. At times I would deny to myself that it ever happened, but in other moments I would come to terms with myself that I did suffer through an evil attack. I needed help from someone who had experience with these things but I didn't know of anyone. You couldn't just look in the yellow pages and find "demonic possession", and I couldn't tell my parents, they would think I was crazy. I didn't know where to turn or who to go to. There wasn't any clinic or place for people to go who suffered through possession. All that I could think about was getting into church. I became curious over what it was that attacked me, but knew that it was an evil spirit of some kind.

I started to go to a church with my first true love that was just being founded by a pastor named Jim who became my first mentor. At times I would visit his home and he would teach me about things on God, the devil, angels and evil spirits. He taught me that what happened to me was called demonic possession and from the sounds of it I was possessed from the moment I entered the occult. He told me that I made an unknown deal with the devil and that these unknowns were the cause of why so many people think there is no problem playing with occult items. There wasn't any sensation or magical event when a demon would possess a person. Most of the time the person didn't feel it and even believe a deliverance minister when they told them they were possessed. Hundreds of thousands of people in this world are possessed and don't even know it. I found out that the reason why the evil spirit that was in me came out was because it wanted to kill everyone there and make it look like I did it, leaving while I went to prison. Unfortunately for the devil it didn't turn out that way because I resisted. I discovered that a demon will stay in a person for a long time waiting for the right opportunity to take over and perform its function. Each evil spirit has a specific function to perform, whether its divination, adultery, blasphemy, or even murder. The problem is trying to discover their purpose and what they intend to do with the person they possess. In order to discover what they intend to do a deliverance minister has to talk to the intelligence of the demon and in so doing play a game of cat and mouse.

Jim was a great guy and a good mentor. I helped him out at times as a youth pastor for his new church. I don't think he had an angry bone in his body. I admired Jim for being a church planter. He built his church for Christ from the ground up. His humble beginnings were out of a school cafeteria where the congregation met every Sunday. At about the time I decided to leave his church they moved to a building that was up for sale just outside of town. The church still meets there to this day. Jim passed away from cancer a year before this book would get published.

After my first true love and I broke up I decided to go to my grandparent's church just north from my mom and dad's new home. It was there that I met Pastor Dwayne who became another mentor for me. He would help me through the periods I had when the spirit tried to come back to me. I could feel the evil spirit trying to reenter my body. So at times I would allow it to try and enter giving it chances just so I could experience what it felt like. It was a eureka moment that I discovered what it felt like when a spirit would try an enter me. I thought that it was important to gain this experience to help others down the road should I happen to come upon someone who has a problem with a demon. I didn't actually believe I would run into anyone else who suffered from possession; I just thought that the experience could help me to identify a real one so someone couldn't take advantage of me. I wanted to be able to identify a true possession from the outside by asking questions on what a person was experiencing so I wasn't taken for a fool. I experienced possession from the inside and I felt that I couldn't afford to lose an opportunity to feel when a demon was trying to enter. By doing this I would be able to tell when possession was taking place and how to prevent it at the start. If I gained this knowledge I would be able to control the demon.

When the spirit would try to reenter me I would feel lightheadedness then feel as if I was going into a trance, also a tingle sensation would run up my spine. Wherever I was I would sit down and clinch my hands into fists and flex my lower back muscles. It was a little trick I learned supernaturally to stay sober during old drinking games. I would stay sober after drinking shots and beer out lasting others but once I lost my concentration I would quickly become drunk. I thought if that trick could keep me sober then it should keep the spirit away. I learnt about chakras and channels during my occult years. I knew that the back was a huge channel and there was a way to close it off from any spirit or unwanted energy. When I began performing deliverances I used this knowledge and would place holy objects behind the possessor's back to cut off any more unwanted spirits from entering their body.

Finally the evil spirit just quit trying to enter me and I never felt it around me again. I believe it was due to all the times I kept going to Sunday service and prayer while it was trying to enter. I concluded that if a person had an evil spirit and kept attending church and fought back the enticement and advances of that spirit, the spirit would grow tired and ultimately leave. If a person's will was strong enough and they resisted then the spirit would leave over time. With that I became a problem solver but there was one problem that always got under my skin that I couldn't figure out.

Like with Pastor Jim, I asked Pastor Dwayne what Psalm 23:1 meant. The both of them informed me that it meant that if we made the Lord our shepherd we wouldn't have to worry or have any want in our lives. I informed the both of them my story behind that verse and how I used to say it before I ever picked up a Bible. They both told me that the Lord wants me to do something. I asked what and they weren't sure, just that I needed to find out.

The unseen world drew my interest and by the time I attended my first years of college I hit the large library and gathered up books on demons, possession and the supernatural. I was that college kid who chose a table and filled it with books, reading in the late hours until the library closed. When the college was hooked up to this new thing called the Internet at the time, I learnt how to surf the web as they called it using the latest search engine called Webcrawler. I looked for all types of names for demons, how they are cast out, where they came from and why they are here. The information I found was shocking. I connected with a lot of the information that appeared to be similar to the experience I went through. I understood that not all possession experiences were the same but I found similarities. I discovered that it is a person's will that pushes a demon out of them. As long as that person doesn't have a will of their own the demon can stay. I recalled this from my experience when the spirit tried to reenter me and remember wanting to push it out, saying to myself that I didn't want this spirit. I felt that it was very old and contributed it to my willingness to want to learn and soak up knowledge. Before my possession I was a "C" student and after the experience I became an "A" student. I soaked up information like a sponge and found myself wanting to learn as much as I could. I still do this today. My friends always tell me that I should go on a game show.

Another key feature I discovered about possession is the fact that I had passed life experiences. I had visions and dreams of myself being a knight, a cowboy and living during several other time periods. I concluded that these were only life signatures as I called it from the people that the spirit had jumped into in the past. The spirit left these marks on my soul when it left suddenly. Some people call this reincarnation but after what I experienced, reincarnation is nothing but crap.

THE CALLING AND BEING TOUCHED BY AN ANGEL

My wife and I built our home and decided on a church to attend. For a short period of time we started attending my old mentor Pastor Dwayne's church. My wife and I were baptized and we moved forward on how to hear from God. We learnt that there were three different ways to hear God from the small still voice that the Prophet Elijah heard to the environment to the audible voice. I've heard people before claim that they heard the audible voice of God. I was skeptical on it but was willing to believe it if it happened to me.

On a Thursday in November, I was taking the trash out to the end of my driveway. Where I lived was way out in the woods, it was quiet and no one was around. Not even a car was driving by. As I reached the end of the drive I looked both ways for any traffic. I was used to no traffic on the road and a sense of peace seemed to fill the air. The birds were chirping and a small breeze blew by. I turned my body around to walk back to the house when a small breeze came up from my left side and went between my left arm and my torso. I quickly paused and heard a voice sounding like a flowing river come out from the breeze. The voice only said my first name. I was instantly filled with energy and peace. I stopped for a moment and kept looking around thinking I could find someone who might have said my name but there was no one around.

As I went back in the house I got my Bible out and began looking for scripture that would tell about the audible voice of God. "Was it God who I heard?" I asked myself. I came upon John 10:27, where it says, "My sheep hear My voice, and I know them, and they follow Me." At that moment I decided to work for God and to build a church for him. I was glad that He built us a home and I wanted to return the favor. So I told him I would build him a house and go to Bible College.

I made a goal to obtain a doctorate in theology and to learn all I could about how to build a church. I started down the long path of theology and read all I could on how to build a church. I wrote up the articles of incorporation, the constitution and bylaws, obtained an FEIN, opened a bank account for the church and formed a board of directors. We started out of our home as a Bible study group but I had a huge vision for the church. It was to evangelize to the teen crowd. The goal was to build a huge church with a stage. A new Christian rock band would play every Sunday. There would be a baptismal pool in the middle of the floor so people could get baptized during concert services. Everyone liked the idea and we began moving forward with it.

One day I was moving some old brush that the contractors left behind from the building of our home when a bee flew out and stung me on my right calf. Over the course of a few days a large black and blue bruise formed around the sting area. I was a little stubborn when people told me I should go see a doctor about it; I just thought it would go away. It took God sending me an angel in a dream one night to tell me to get some ointment on the sting area. In my dream it was dark and a man with his arms crossed came out of the darkness wearing a green shirt and a red hat. He looked at me then looked down at my leg and informed me that I needed to get ointment on my leg or else I would lose it. I woke up and told my wife about the dream I had and she convinced me that it was God trying to tell me to get it checked out. After church we drove to the nearest urgent care where the doctor had looked at my leg and prescribed me antibiotics and some ointments. A line started to form that was following a vein up my leg. My wife spoke up and asked the doctor if I let it go would I have lost my leg? The doctor informed us that if I was foolish enough to let it go I might have.

As I studied in Bible College I came to find out that angels will enter your dreams and warn you of things or even prepare a path for you in your journey. In Genesis Jacob fell asleep and saw angels ascending and descending on a ladder that led to Heaven. I noticed that in that story that it didn't say "descending and ascending," it said "ascending and descending." The angels of God are already on earth working and keeping those who do the Lord's work of the Gospel safe.

ATTACKS AND WARNINGS
FROM THE DEMONIC

After my first deliverance session on the witch girl case I went out with Pastor Bill on the streets. We went from one town, where there were sightings of witches and rumors of witches doing things in the woods, to a college town. We were open air preaching when a man walked up to Bill and was talking to him. I watched from across the street as the man suddenly began getting in Bill's face. Bill pointed at him and kept saying, "Get behind me Satan!" He obviously saw something in the man. The man backed away from Bill and walked across the street to me and began pointing at me saying, "That goes for you too!" From my teachings I recognized the man having widening eyes and grinning and quickly identified him as possibly possessed. "You're on notice!" he said as I began to laugh at him. He walked away crossing the street he came from and passing Bill. I watched the man walk far down the street only to stop, put his hand up to his head, shaking it and turned to look at us. I knew then that the man was possessed and the devil wanted to give us a message to stop what we were doing. As the loving stubborn Christians we were we didn't listen to the warning and continued to lead people to Christ.

At the time we made a plan to evangelize every Saturday night on the college streets of the old town section. We each had a corner and would open air preach. Some people blew shofars and walked up and down the streets talking with people. We gave people the Law of God, convicted them of sin so they could see they offended a just and holy God and gave them the gospel message of salvation. We did this lovingly toward people. Sometimes the message wasn't received very well and we had to turn the other cheek. I was personally honored with spit, ice water thrown at me, pushes, curses, people following me to try and beat me up and snow balls. But we kept going out to take a stand against the devil and bring people to Christ and boy did we send a message and did we ever bring people to Christ. I can't say that all of this didn't come without sacrifice though. There were times when I came home at 3 A.M. in the morning in tears from what people said to me. I would suck it up and move on. I began to understand the feelings that Jesus had as he took each step toward the cross. Each night I evangelized, talked one on one with people and listened to atheists, evolutionists, agnostics and people of other religions come against me. They would challenge me and I became emotionally drained and spiritually weakened. Still I took the steps as slow as they came and mustered all my energy to keep moving just as Christ took steps through the streets of Jerusalem. There were even the deliverances on the side that took an emotional strain on my being. Each time I would pluck out a demon from a person in Jesus name it felt as if a piece of me was being sacrificed. I'd feel drained, tired and beat down. The once man who fell head over heels for God was slowly being drained and the smile started to turn upside down. I fully realized the life that Jesus promised Christians was real. The world would come at us, torment us, and try to destroy us; but still we needed to fight the good fight and show our light with a positive attitude. Being the salt of the earth and giving the Law and the gospel message. But that was just it. There was so much pain and suffering from people on the streets and everywhere I talked with people while giving the Law, God's Ten Commandments, was like pouring salt on an open wound. It hurt people; angered them and even more people would come out to challenge us even though we still turned our cheeks and loved on them. We offered help, food, prayer and a shoulder to cry on. People would come down from their homes, apartments and seek out prayer and healing. We didn't do all of this for ourselves but for them. To show people just how much Jesus loved them we sacrificed by going out in below zero weather. Most of the people who argued or tormented us would return later in tears and ask how they could accept Jesus as their savior. Of course we would show them how. One of the most beautiful sights was to know that Pastor John took advantage of the river nearby in full view of people and would baptize anyone who wanted to be.

We continued to evangelize on the streets of the college town. I even open air preached in front of an abortion clinic. We walked down the frat and sorority houses during parties and brought more people to Christ. The devil sent us more atheists and evolutionists to come against us on the streets but we brought them to Christ also. I use to be an atheist so I knew what they were thinking. I would tell them that the only reason why they were atheists was the fear of knowing that if there was a God that they wouldn't be able to do what they wanted to do; so they shut God out completely.

Then the devil started giving me loud messages to stop what I was doing. One day I was putting the dishes away while my wife was working. I was home alone and I had kitchen drawers open. I placed silverware away and walked back to the sink when the drawer slammed shut. One night while we were watching a movie on television in our living room an unseen force held me down to the floor and wouldn't let me back up. It took my wife and myself prayer to force the spirit off me. But we continued to sacrifice and go back out on the streets and bring people to Christ. Another night while we were asleep I woke up to hearing three loud poundings on our master bathroom door. I looked at the clock and it read three fifteen a.m. This was the Forth Watch. The period of the night when prophecy could be obtained and when the spirits were more pronounced.

At one point I was sleeping when I woke up to a hag-like shadowy face in front of me, face to face. I watched as the black shadowy form bolted out of the room, causing the kitchen light to flicker on and off and giving out a loud screech. In a split second my dog jumped off the bed and ran after the shadow. I quickly woke my wife up and told her what I saw. The next day when we awoke I cleansed the house with holy incense and blessed it. Since that attack for a week I would come home late at night while working second shift to hear loud screeches the moment I would walk up the steps to my house. The noises would come from the woods behind the house and sometimes from across the road. I contributed this to a possible owl but the sound of the screech was too similar to the one that came from the shadow in my home.

For a period of six years while doing deliverance ministry and casting out demons there wasn't any attacks. One March morning I was driving home from my job, working third shift, when I suddenly blacked out and regained my consciousness just in time to turn the steering wheel to the right, allowing me to hit the guard rail. The car rode the rail, ripping off a rear tire, and then spun in a circle sliding down the freeway to a grassy area. There was debris everywhere. I recall thinking while the car was in a spin that this was it, that the devil finally got his wish for me to die. The devil wanted nothing more than to get rid of me; to stop the salvations and deliverances our ministry was bringing. When the car came to a halt I shook my head and watched as cars went by. I couldn't believe what just happened. How could I have been so foolish as to fall asleep at the wheel? But the Lord was looking out for me. I was so pumped full of adrenaline that I unhooked my seat belt and walked out of the car. I looked at the amount of damage to the car and was in disbelief. The whole front of the car was smashed in, a tire on the rear was ripped off with the side ripped open like a tin can, and the back end was destroyed. I thought to myself, "How can I be alive?" Not only did the Lord save me from the crash but sent me two nurses who were driving by. One of them called 911 for emergency while the other led me back into the car to sit back down. I began to complain of a neck pain as my adrenaline wore off. When the firefighters, police and EMT's arrived they had to take me out on a stretcher since I had some neck pain. The EMT that was talking with me in the ambulance informed me that the firefighters told him that if I wouldn't have turned right before the crash I probably wouldn't have made it. To the left of the end of the guard rail was Mud Creek. If I wouldn't have turned my steering left I would have went off a small cliff loaded with tree trunks on the way down. It seems that in my life the devil will always try to secretly do something to me but the Lord would always send me aid. I believe that day the Lord woke me up just in time to turn my steering wheel. As I recall the event, I remember the feeling of being pressed back in my seat upon impact as the car spun; it wasn't the seat belt or the airbag that held me in.

A year later the year from hell came upon us. Not long after the beginning of the year my father passed away, a hero from the Vietnam War. His funeral was honorable. I've been to a lot of funerals in my life but this one touched my heart. I recall turning down the dirt road going to the cemetery, where much of my family is buried, and looking to the right to see how many cars were following us. I swear the train of cars must have gone for five miles or more.

At my father's funeral, for the first time I was able to see myself in the mirror and how God had molded me into the man I am today. My old mentor Pastor Dwayne had given the funeral proceedings and he shocked the people attending when he informed them that I was going to say a few words. I wanted to show people how noble this man, my father, was and how strong he raised his two sons. I thought that by me giving a small speech I could give strength to my family during this time of mourning. This is what I spoke to the people attending his funeral.

"The Australian poet Pam Brown once said, 'Dads are most ordinary men turned by love into heroes, adventurers, story tellers and singer of songs.'

This was so true of my brother and I's father. Dad would hardly talk of Vietnam but when he would talk to us about the war we would get him on a role so we could visualize his adventures and see the hero in him. He is our hero.

Proverbs 23:24 says, 'The father of a righteous child has great joy; a man who fathers a wise son rejoices in him.' Through my brother and I's endeavors in sports, dating, marriage and careers, I knew by the joy on dad's face that he rejoiced and was glad in us; especially when we left home.

The great psycho-therapist Sigmund Freud said, 'I cannot think of any need in childhood as strong as the need for a father's protection.' Thank you dad for being our protector and for teaching us what is right and what is wrong.

I leave you all with these words from God's divine Law. Exodus 20:12 says, 'Honor your father and your mother, so that you may live long in the land the Lord your God is giving you.'"

I went through a long period of depression after my father passed away. In a way it was a knockout punch that the devil gave me. I called a meeting of our board of directors together and discussed with them some topics and issues. Taking ecclesiastical power, I asked for a vote to dissolve our church. The board agreed and the vote was unanimous; our church was shut down.

I was broken and beaten. I had fought the devil and his demons, giving victory after victory to the Lord and giving Him the glory. But I know what you are saying, "Why give up?" I wasn't giving up even though it looked like I was. You see our board of directors saw that the church was holding me back like a lion trapped in a cage. The board felt that I could do more by not being bound to the church. No one wanted to take over as the bishop of the church and since my wife and I built the church the board agreed to dissolve it. In some ways I felt free and could do more for the Lord.

A few months after my father passed away his sister informed us that she had a rare form of cancer. The doctors had asked her if she wanted to do chemo but being the stubborn Christian woman she was told the doctor to give it to her straight. Treatment for this rare form of cancer was useless they told her. She accepted it and knew that the Lord was calling her home. She decided to go back home and await death.

I visited her in her home to say good bye and told her I loved her. This woman who brought me to Christ and who fought to bring her family to the cross passed away. She was the last of the children of my grandparents. All I had left on my father's side was my grandmother. She had watched her husband and all three of her children pass away one by one over the course of ten years.

Three months went by and my mother and I visited my grandmother at the nursing home she was staying. By this time the loss of her husband and children had taken a toll on her. She had a small stroke after her son, my father, died and when I was walking through the halls of the nursing hall with my mother I couldn't help but wonder if she was going to recognize me. I walked in to greet her roommate and see my grandmother sleeping in her bed. My mother woke her up and she saw me. She greeted me and said my name. A relief came over me as she smiled. She was happy to see me. I greeted her and we talked as I raised my voice for her to hear me. She asked me to look in the bottom drawer of her dresser telling me that there was a book for me. As the respectful grandson I was I opened the bottom drawer and spotted a blue Bible. I saw no other books but was thinking that she was going to give me a book on the genealogy of our family due to our conversation. "There is only a blue Bible grandma." I informed her. "Yes, that is for you." She replied and informed me that that was the Bible that my father and mother gave her and my grandfather when they decided to go to church. At that moment all I could do was look at it. It was as if she wanted to tell me that she would be okay and that God was speaking through her to tell me to stand and keep going. After my visit with my grandmother a few weeks went by and she passed away. My father's whole side, my grandfather, grandmother, uncle and aunt were now all gone.

In some ways I wanted to walk up the stairs to heaven and punch God in the face for all I went through. But my training, education and experience as a minister of the gospel of Jesus Christ told me that it wasn't His fault. The real blame was upon humanity, all the way back in the garden; when Adam & Eve made the choice to sin, affecting the rest of us. Mankind was the one who invited death into God's creation, not God. Death is a foreigner. God's nature is life not death. Can you imagine what we put God through? Because of Adam & Eve's sin God was now forced into being a judge because there is no one higher than him to judge. He is a loving God but we made him judge over us. I had no right to blame God for the death of family members, attacks and such. The full blame was upon myself and humanity for missing the mark and trespassing on supernatural territory that is not our own. And because of it we make ourselves debtors to supernatural beings that we cannot pay back except with our own lives. It took God himself to come down to our level in the form of Jesus to save us.

I don't truly know if the devil had a hand in my losses but I do know that he used those experiences against me. I knew that he wanted to make me feel depressed and dwell on the possibility that there wasn't any hope. I knew better than that. I let the word richly dwell in me longer than he may think. Though I was at my lowest point in my life, the Lord would give me hope.

THE ASCENSION

Prior to the passing of my father, I had fallen asleep in my bed. When I awoke I was fully conscious and standing in a wheat field. I was by myself but didn't feel alone. I looked around and could see a night sky and edge of a galaxy in bright contrasting colors. The wheat field's color was a bright color of yellow and orange. As I walked through the field I felt at complete peace and enjoyment. I felt at home.

I could feel the wind as it moved passed my body and skipped along the heads of the wheat causing them to bend. My eyes took in the whole place and I couldn't believe how beautiful the land was. I never thought once about how I got there or any of my loved ones. All I could think about was the joy and peace I received from the place. I wanted so much to not move, so I laid down on the ground in the wheat field and starred up at the night sky. The stars were of all different kinds of colors and the edge of the galaxy was beautiful. I heard a voice tell me to get up because there was more to see. I stood up and looked around to see a single tree in the field. Its green high contrast leaves were beautiful and glittering. I didn't walk to it but was rather led to a creek nearby. I came to the edge of the creek and walked down to it and noticed how still the water was. The water was a cyan-like color, beautiful and high contrast. As the water flowed with nearly no sound it was also captured in a nearby puddle that looked like a well. I formed my hand into a cup and dipped into the water. It was cool to the touch and when I drank the water it was refreshing. I felt alive instantly and strength came to me. I stood up and heard the voice again speak to me, telling me it was time to go back.

When I came to in my bed I quickly sat up and found myself in tears. I was balling my eyes out. I felt as if a piece of my soul was torn from me. It took me a moment to realize where I was. I was back in my house in bed. The sun was shining through the window and I just starred outside to see the view of the trees in the front lawn. I quickly became depressed and felt as if I was in a foreign land even though I was home. I got out of bed and went to the sink to splashed water in my face and caught a whiff of the iron well water that we used out in the country. Though I have been drinking the country water for years without any trouble it was hard for me to swallow. I wondered where I was just then while I looked at myself in the mirror. I felt like I was teleported some how. My psychology training kicked in and I quickly tried to put it off as if I was hallucinating but I couldn't. The experience was too real to ignore. It literally felt like I was somewhere else. As a theologian I knew that God would allow people to visit heaven at times. So I asked myself, "Was I just in heaven?"

I knew that the Apostle Paul talked about a man who either in the body or not, he wasn't sure, had visited heaven (2 Corinthians 12:2). Other Christians have had the same experience at times. It is called *ascending*, and is a right for all Christians to have the ability to do. God allowed me to have a taste of heaven and the experience was so moving that I had to share it with others. I told family members and friends; and when my aunt was dying of cancer I told her what heaven was like so she knew what awaited her. She spoke of my good bye visit for days to others who visited her on her death bed.

I can honestly say that I experienced both heaven and hell but the hell I experienced was a literal place. What I had experienced was the devil's attacks upon my life, and I heard horror stories from others who have actually visited a place like hell. The sure presence of a demon itself is the edge of hell. When we experience the presence of a demon we smell either rotting flesh, sulfur, urine or feces. That is what hell smells like from the experiences I've heard from others; along with the feeling that there is no strength in your body and no hope.

I am glad to share with you my ascending experience but my question for you is this. Would you rather live an eternity in heaven or an eternity in hell? God doesn't send you to one or the other place, you send yourself to one of those places. You should not be concerned with the events and struggles of this life but be more concerned on how to be with God. He who is born once dies twice, but he who is born twice dies once. Keep in mind that should you decide to take yourself to hell that you will die twice. You will die bodily and you will die spiritually, being forever separated from God; this is the second death.

tHE HAt

In 1882, Victorien Sardou performed a play that was written by Sarah Bernhardt. The play was titled *Fédora*; which was about a heroine princess who wore an interesting hat. In the late 19th century a new hat was born that grew to become the fashion model for female hat bearing. It was the fedora, which quickly grew to become a male fashion statement. The hat was known to be able to protect the wearers head from rain and wind.

In the early 20th century Orthodox Jews began to wear black fedoras with their daily attire, and by the 1920's the fedora became a popular icon. Today it is best known for the period of prohibition and the great depression.

The fedora has a romantic sense about it and is a symbol of style and status. Today, we don't see many of the hats around. By the late 1950's the hat began to lose favor over more fashionable and comfortable form fitting clothing. However, by the mid 1970's the fedora enjoyed a small period of popularity with the style changes but again went away. By the early 1980's when the Indiana Jones movies premiered in theaters the fedora grew in popularity again and each time gaining attention with each new sequel.

Up until the late 90's and early 2000's the hat had faded away again until swing was in. Kids and young adults met at dance floors and took lessons on how to swing. But that too faded away as did the fedora.

The fedora for years has been a hat that comes and goes like a tide in the moving waves of time. People use the hat for a period then place it in a treasure chest and pack it away in the attic. It's almost like a grandfather passes away and a grand kid receives an inheritance and opens the chest to find the hat with the years going by. The grand kid loved the grandfather so much that he wears the hat periodically until he gets tired of it and places it in his closet only to use it again when he gets older, to of coarse impress the girls.

People often ask me why I wear the fedora, while receiving tons of compliments on my hat. If you don't know, I wear a black fedora and tip it to one side. To most people it seems to be a mystery to see a man in a collar wearing a black fedora. I'd walk into stores, homes, events, conferences, conventions and such and people would always stop and stare at me. Their mouths open always starring at the hat. I love that hat. Not because of what it does but what it means and the period from which it comes from. You see the early 20th century was always my favorite time period. I loved the 1950's and loved the idea that I knew someone in my life that was a teenager during the 50's; my aunt who helped me see Christ. But that isn't the reason why I wear the black fedora. I wear the hat out of mockery of the devil. Each time I wear the black fedora I personally am mocking Satan and his demons. Why? There are a lot of reports from people who have said that they see shadow people wearing what looks like a 1920's era hat. Well, that is a fedora. I wanted a tool to wear on my person, a symbol that would mock the devil personally but yet would show a symbol of authority. As a quiet person I would always have my conversations butted in or be patronized. When I was dealing with demons I didn't want confusion, I wanted attention away from confusion because I knew that God is not the author of confusion. As a student of psychology I decided on a roostering method of gaining control in events where demons were present. Psychologists call this method roostering due to the rooster's ability of taking charge over female chickens easily. The rooster is colorful and has a large red comb on its head that gives it automatic authority over other chickens. The roostering method states that anyone who wears something that is out of place from the rest of the crowd they obtain attention and are seen as an automatic figure of authority. The last thing I wanted during deliverance sessions was chaos over who would lead. I didn't need some young or inexperienced person telling me what I should and shouldn't do. So after carefully looking over symbols to wear on my person I came across the story of *The Shadow*.

The Shadow was created on July 31, 1930 by Street & Smith Publications for Detective Story Magazine. It quickly got on the air waves as a radio show and became popular.

The Shadow was none other than Lamont Cranston who learnt how to alter the perceptions of men's minds. Lamont used to be an evil man himself and understood the concept behind it. From his years of being a criminal warlord in Asia he would rob, war and rule over men as an evil tyrant. One day a master of mind control took him in as an apprentice and changed Lamont for the better; you could say he saved Lamont's soul. Lamont traveled home to his native United States where he decided to use his new powers to bend men's minds and fight crime. He decided to become *The Shadow*; a symbol of the darkness of men coming against them. He began to fight against mobs, crime lords and super villains wearing a black cloak with red lining, a red scarf over his mouth and a black fedora. Lamont knew evil and the old phrase that followed The Shadow was, *"Who knows what evil lurks in the hearts of men? The Shadow knows."*

When I came out of possession and discovered The Shadow I grew to like him because I could relate with the character of Lamont. He had seen evil, did it and understood it enough to fight against it. I was an occultist, suffered through possession, came out of it and understood the devil enough to come against him and fight him. So for me the hat became a symbol, a memorial of what I went through. A mockery of the devil that I am still here, living and breathing, a thorn in his side; bringing others to the cross of Christ and the real superhero who is Jesus himself.

THE ANGEL OF BLACK MAGICK

In March of 2009 I received a telephone call from a paranormal team based in Grayling, Michigan who would handle cases throughout the Mid Michigan and Northern Michigan areas. They were the Mid Michigan Paranormal Investigators operated by Matt and Melanie Moyer who needed a demonologist to look into a case in Holly, Michigan. They had had a terrible experience with a previous demonologist that they worked with, so I agreed to help. I heard a lot of positive things about the team and looked forward to working with them.

One of the founders called me, whose name was Matt. My first impression of Matt was that he was an authority figure. We talked for what seemed like an hour on the phone about the case. Our conversation was about a haunting that was going on between their client's house and the client's store. The case was about a woman who married a widower and moved into his home. She began to experience activity that she thought was her husband's ex-wife. In the beautiful old home there was a room upstairs that his wife resided in until her passing. She had died from an illness and upon her passing the husband left things the way they were in the room and closed the door. He asked his new wife and her son not enter the room. She had agreed, however when mysterious circumstances surrounding the room and her son occurred she had thought that she was going insane. A ghost of a woman began to appear to her son first and then to her. She contributed the ghost to being her husband's ex-wife until she saw a woman at the top of the stairs with a boy wearing Victorian era clothing. She knew then that the ghost wasn't her husband's ex-wife. When she began to work at the antique store with her husband, her and an assistant began to experience the haunt there as well. At one point she had went into the basement and spotted a lizard-like humanoid that appeared depressed. Other appearances in the store and the house showed that the apparitions of the spirits revealed missing limbs. The paranormal team began to believe that this haunting was actually demonic.

The team didn't have any experience with demonic cases at the time but knew how to spot one and had spoken with a woman who was connected to demonology out east. She had informed them that what they were dealing with was a lower class demon. Matt had also contacted my friend and demonologist Tracy Bacon who agreed that it was a lower form of demon. Tracy suggested to Matt to contact for the case. Many people believe that there are two classes of demons and they define them as uppers and lowers. However, as a pastor who came from the Christian church and I go by what the Bible said. I classified the demonic in their various forms from evil spirits to unclean spirits (which were actually "impure spirits" upon possession or *spiritus immundus* in Latin; *pneuma akatharton* in the Greek) all the way to devils. I treated devils and evil spirits as the same thing but some in the paranormal used the word "devil" to represent higher end demons. I didn't follow the paranormal lingo. I was from the Christian Church and we did things differently. When dealing with the big boy demons I didn't call them "uppers", my brothers in Christ and I called them *principalities*, *powers*, *rulers of the darkness* of this world, and spiritual wickedness in *high places*. I knew an exorcist who cast out an *evil spirit* out of a man in Lansing and when he did the man's boots flew off; who knew it was a minor demon. My point is the Christian Churches knowledge of the classification of demons was much wider. To me the lower and upper idea was for beginners. The church, as a whole, treats even false gods, fallen angels, jinn and other foreign ideas as demons as well. These are either religious or deceptive spirits whose sole purpose is to deceive humanity.

I decided to help hunt this possible demon down and agreed to meet Matt and his team at the antique shop in Holly. I was told that there would be two authors who were also historians there who agreed to write the victims story down. These historians were Kathleen Tedsen and Beverlee Rydel. I was rather impressed when I met them as they informed me of the history of the antique store and how the house used to sit on a property that was owned by a man who performed incest on his niece. She had a son and when the authorities discovered what had happened the uncle was tried in court for incest.

From the beginning the case appeared to me that there was a spirit moving between the store and the house; or several of them. I instantly knew that in order for that to happen the spirit had to be connected to a person; I kept this in mind while driving down to Holly to meet with the team and the historians. The last time I had visited Holly was with Ray. I recalled how Ray had informed me that the

Holly Hotel was haunted but I didn't believe it at the time. I was curious though and always wanted to visit the hotel and check it out.

I arrived in Holly early and decided to first drive around the town to get a feel for the area and discern it. To me it felt like any other small town. It had a hint of mystery to it. Since I arrived early I felt that I would experience a rush of people, but there wasn't anyone around. The town felt alive but had a lack of people walking about it at the time. It was like a ghost town with people. Of course I knew that the town residence had left for the evening but most other small towns I visited had at least cars driving through; Holly did not. I parked my car and began to walk around the town and I felt like I was the only one there. I watched as birds flew overhead and landed in a tree. I was standing on new cement making up a sidewalk corner, which gave a sense of newness to the town. The town itself was beautiful but I was just shocked over the lack of street traffic. Suddenly a single car drove by and exited out of town. For a moment I felt stupid for staring at the car as it came in and went. They probably saw this man who was wearing a black fedora, tan jacket and black slacks, thinking I was a police officer looking for people who were walking the streets passed curfew.

I decided to walk back to my car, put the seat back and take a nap. I did so and set the alarm on my cell phone to wake up in just enough time to start the car up and drive a little ways to the store. I found a large parking lot, kicked back the seat, put my hat over my eyes and fell asleep. When I awoke I looked at my cell phone clock to notice I was actually now running late. My phone was on vibrate and the alarm had went off but I didn't hear it. I didn't have any coffee but I knew a technique that would quickly wake me up so I wasn't groggy when I arrived at the store. I opened my door up and began breathing in deep. I was asthmatic and knew that if I breathed in too much oxygen that I would be energized and wake up like a person drinking caffeinated coffee. I felt a rush and was awake and alert now. I got back in my car, started it and drive to the store.

When I arrived I stayed in my car to gather a few things and collect my thoughts. I had fasted that day and felt my stomach rumble and drank only water to keep myself hydrated. I took a sip of water from my water bottle and watched a few of the investigators from Matt's team walking by and entering the store. I watched as they were setting things up and people from the team were walking around. They didn't know me and I sat there wondering what might happen. I was into exposing the devil and his demons to the public. I figured why not, Jesus had a public deliverance ministry why can't I? As an evangelist I thought it was a great tool to show people a deliverance to help strengthen a person's faith; and boy did it ever work. It seemed where ever I went a demon would pop out to confront me or if it didn't I would find it and remove it. I was curious if this team was ready for a demonic exposure.

I opened the door to my car and stepped out avoiding a puddle, fixed my hat and opened the back door to gather my things. At this time I wondered if the people inside were looking out the window wondering if the person in the black hat was their demonologist. I was a little nervous and looked up through the window to see that no one looking in my direction. A sense of relief came over me. I grabbed my bag of tricks as I liked to call it and opened the bag. I made sure that all my things were in order, the holy water, anointing oils, prayer book, and most importantly my binder with the oaths of exorcism. As I moved things around I heard the familiar sound of Christmas bells and looked down to find the Orthodox incense burner. The chains on the incense burner had round bells that when moved would give the familiar tone of Christmas bells. The Holy Spirit came over me and I felt that something was going to happen that night. Rather than take the burner with me I decided to leave it in the car as a last resort. The burner was like placing a bomb in a home with demonic activity. A hot coal is placed inside and holy incense was placed on top of the hot coal, then smoke would begin to leak out filling every place with the holy fire. The Holy Spirit taught me to use the holy smoke while praying in each room of a house. He had led me to the hidden knowledge that the heart and the gull were taken out from a fish, pierced through on a stick of incense and roasted over a fire and put out. For some odd reason demons didn't like this and were driven away. I asked the Holy Spirit which led me to the knowledge on why this technique drove out demons. The Lord would tell me that the technique was symbolic of the spear that pierced the side of Jesus while on the cross. The spear pierced through Jesus' liver and went up into his heart. The image at that moment in time was the victory over the forces of evil. The Lord taught me that by using the holy incense while saying a prayer of obedience reminded demons of the victory, "It is finished." I was stunned and decided to have our church purchase an incense burner. Each case I used the burner the victims of the haunt would report back that the activity would stop. The key to this knowledge was knowing that the smoke from the incense symbolized prayers. If a person surrounds themselves with Jesus just as the smoke from the incense burner would fill their house, the demon that haunted them would leave.

As I entered the store I announced myself to Melanie who was one of the lead investigators of the paranormal team. She showed me around the store helping me to identify the areas where the spirits were seen. She introduced me to the rest of her team and I had greeted Matt also. I was impressed over their style of professionalism but Melanie was looking to me to lead the investigation. I respectfully declined and only wanted to observe the case until I was able to identify something demonic. I wanted them to do what they traditionally did while I watched from the background to find anything odd. This was my usual tactic when hunting down demons. I figured the devil can act like a lion why can't I? After all my families crest was given to my ancestors by Richard the Lion Heart. Our symbol was the lion and our motto "Sans Peur" was French for "Without Fear." After my possession I wasn't afraid of demons or anything dark anymore. Because of it I wanted to display my families honor with the motto on our hearts and give it to others where fear was ruling their lives. My mission in deliverance ministry was to turn fear into faith. It worked.

The store was very interesting. One of the main things that stuck out as I recall the case was the wall of Nazi Germany items. There were helmets, hats, medals and insignias and various swastikas.

Another thing was the vampire killing kit in the back of the store. As I looked around more closely my eyes began to widen at the thought of the amount of items from around the world. In some ways as a lover of history and culture I felt in heaven. However, I couldn't help but to think of what type of spirits could be attached to these items. I felt a little overwhelmed when I thought of the possibility of multiple spirits being involved in this place.

I greeted the authors/historians and talked with them more about their books and why they were there. Bev and Kat told me how they were tagging along with paranormal teams and recording the haunts in historical locations. When I greeted the owners I quickly was taken by them. The Hays were a lovely couple. The husband Mark had lost his wife after she passed away and later married Lynn. We talked about their case and discussed how she thought that the ghost in their house might have been Mark's ex-wife; but later didn't believe it was due to the Victorian clothing. What I found most interesting was the reptilian humanoid she saw in the basement of the store. I asked her to show me and we went down with a few investigators into the store's basement.

When we arrived in the basement I noticed an old brick wall and hole to get to the other side. The brick wall and the old wood floor upstairs revealed how old the building was. Lynn pointed in the hole and informed me that was the place she saw the reptilian creature as an apparition. She said it looked sad and had black eyes. I requested that she draw me a picture of what she saw. This was common practice in deliverance ministry to have someone who saw a demon recall and draw it. We can then connect to folklore and legends that surround the area. She informed me how that if it stood up it would appear fourteen feet tall. My mind quickly went back to the nephilim of Genesis 6:1-4. As she described the creature in more detail experience told me that it was demonic but I wasn't going to be quick about mentioning that. I wanted to see more. I was convinced that what the owners were dealing with was demonic but I wanted to know its weaknesses and how it got into their lives. I didn't want to startle them and cause fear, so I did the best I could to be professional about informing them what I believed they were up against.

I asked if either one of them had performed anything of the occult and gave examples. She mentioned that her and a friend, when they were young, had written on a paper with their blood by puncturing their fingers with toothpicks, giving their souls to the devil. She mentioned that they did this in hopes that the devil would get back at the teachers in school for abusing students. They proceeded to bury their contracts in the backyard and they went to bed. When they awoke they realized the silliness of what they did and went into the backyard to dig up their contracts. When they turned the soil over to get their contracts back they were gone. She then asked me if that meant anything. At this time my mouth had dropped and I was amazed over what I heard. I didn't hesitate to inform her that her soul was still owned by the devil due to that contract. "The Devil has those contracts." I informed her. She was in a little bit of disbelief over it all until I informed her that I had seen demons move objects and teleport objects out of locked safes. I then asked her if she had received any type of abuse in her past. She proceeded to inform me of some personal experiences that happen to her. I didn't say anymore to anyone. I knew then what was up and how the demon got into their lives. I informed the couple of the seriousness of their situation. Lynn had thought that by accepting Jesus as her Lord and Savior her past would be cleaned up. I told Lynn that is just what the devil wants us to believe. I told her that our sins are forgiven when we accept Christ but the devil will hold onto the legal issues of our past. She was in shock that her past use of black magick could affect present events. I informed the couple that the devil acts like an attorney walking this world grabbing up rights that we drop. When we make a contract with the devil, no matter how much as children we think it is silly, the devil will honor it. We foolishly believe that small silly things that we do in our lives can't possibly invite demonic activity; but they can. We may think that they are forgotten but the devil always digs up the past and snakes his way through the endless piles of legal documents to have his way with us. After my conversation with the Hays couple the paranormal team began to pack a few of their things to head over to the house.

When we arrived at the home I noticed how beautiful it was. It had that historic feel added to the area. The house was romantic with a pond in the background and antiques out front that gave it character. We were invited inside and were instantly in the living area. To the left was an office area and a stairway that led up to the bedrooms. Matt led me through the house and down into the basement there was more antiques. A part of me wanted to contribute to the idea that the antiques in the store and in the house may have some kind of connection. Still I wanted to wait it out and see what else I could find. I only sat back and observed for a while. When things began to settle down and the team split up, Matt took a few teammates to the store while the rest stayed with Melanie and I. Lynn's husband had left with Matt's team to go to the store, while Lynn stayed with us at the house. I began talking with Lynn for a while and we connected. I really liked her personality and where she came from. I wanted to help her through her haunting and told myself to stay committed to helping her and her family.

I decided that now was the right time to expose where the demon was. It was as if I could see it because I knew where it was. I knew where he or they were hiding. I could see them spiritually and was a little disgusted that they were hiding. I knew from the manner they were acting that nothing was going to happen during the team's investigation, so I decided to expose them like in a game of Clue. I didn't say anything to draw attention to where they were hiding. It was like a game of chess in a way or the ending of a comic book where the villain's true intension was exposed. I let everything play out among the paranormal team and the historians. They or he were in Lynn and hiding very well. As I began to talk with Lynn I noticed that our conversation was being secretly recorded and watched. She had just got done drawing what the demon in the basement looked like. She showed me an image of a lizard-like creature squatting. The lizard man had a comb on top of its head and appeared very thin. I definitely knew then that this was a demon.

I tried to ignore the cameras of the historians and their writing and concentrated on just helping Lynn. She and I talked more about the contract she had made with the devil. I asked her if she could do something for me and write out a new contract that would make the contract she made with the devil null and void. She agreed and I proceeded to tell her what she needed to write. She began to take down what I was telling her but then suddenly stopped when I asked her to write, *"... and I renounce Satan"*. She couldn't move. He began to receive a ringing in her ears and couldn't hear me. I took out my anointing oil and put the sign of the cross over her ears saying, "I circumcise your spiritual ears now in Jesus name, and command whatever spirit that is oppressing Lynn to stop now." She looked up at me and told me that the ringing was gone. She fought hard to finish out the rest of the new contract with God, signed her name and she immediately received a headache. I quickly grabbed the new contract and asked God to make the previous contract Lynn made with the devil null and void and to honor this new one. I anointed the contract with the seal of the cross of Christ, then turned to Lynn and placed the sign of the cross on her forehead. Her headache was now gone. I led her over to the couch when I noticed that one of Melanie's teammates got out a thermo imager and began to scan for heat signatures. Lynn and I talked about the black magick she used to do and I asked her if she was willing to renounce it. She agreed and began to repeat everything I said renouncing the black magick she did. When she was done she received a mysterious stomach pain. I knew then that she was demon possessed and they were hiding well. She asked for a drink of water and I exited with Melanie to the kitchen where she proceeded to get a glass. I requested her to get a plastic cup instead and informed her that if Lynn is possessed with a demon that I didn't want to be cut by glass. She filled the plastic cup with water and I asked to hold it. I blessed the water as the blood of Christ and handed it back to Melanie. I informed Melanie that if Lynn were truly possessed then she should have a negative reaction to the holy water. She went in and handed it to Lynn who drank the water made holy and began to have a stomach ache. I knew for certain then that she was possessed and Melanie looked at me in amazement.

I asked Lynn to stand up and together we began to command the evil spirits in her to come out in Jesus name. I commanded the spirit to give me its name. The spirit responded through her saying its name was Pianna. I placed the Bible into her belly and commanded in authority for the demons to come out of her, informing them that they no longer had any right over Lynn. She quickly ran to the bathroom and proceeded to vomit.

As we sat there talking with Kat and Bev while Lynn was in the bathroom we soon began to hear a loud growl sound, then the sound of two small animals fighting. We ran to the stairway leading down stairs where a house cat had begun to hiss at us. The evil spirits that came out of Lynn had gone into the cats and began fighting among themselves. Lynn had informed us that the cats never fought or hissed at people. I looked at Lynn and she was pale skinned. She told me how she felt weak and dehydrated. They were all too familiar symptoms of what I and others who I helped through demonic possession. I requested that she get a sports drink to replace the electrolytes she lost. My first concern was the dehydration that people experience after deliverance. Next she needed energy so she needed something to eat and I advised that she eat some crackers so it wouldn't hurt her stomach.

After the deliverance, Melanie and Matt decided to get the team back together at the store. We all met at the store and Matt told us about the experiences that he had. He was deathly afraid of spiders and while in the basement, near the location that Lynn had seen the creature, he had experienced what felt like spiders hatching over his head and running down his head in the dark. He actually thought that there were spiders on him until a teammate shined a light and revealed that there was nothing to be seen. He mentioned how it felt as if the spirit knew his inner phobia and used it against him. This happened at nearly the same time as the deliverance at the house; but what was most interesting was the EVP they obtained at the moment the evil spirits were cast out. They had received an EVP of a spirit saying, "Satan" and another one "Pianna". There wasn't any way for Matt to know the name of the spirit at the house. Matt and his teammates were three to four miles away at the store. The only communication the teams had was through walkie talkie but there was complete radio silence during that time.

Matt's experience at the store was extraordinary. The EVP's they got and his personal experience were evidence that the deliverance at the house was genuine. There wasn't any way that the name Pianna could have come up in both locations at the same time.

I asked if Lynn and her husband needed anything else. She mentioned that she was feeling better. I blessed her and her husband in Jesus name and bid the team good bye and left.

Weeks later I received a call from Matt who had informed me that the Hays were doing well. The apparitions stopped and there weren't any signs of any supernatural activity. I was relieved to hear it. It is always any deliverance ministers fear that a haunting continues after they've been there. The idea that a demon hasn't left leaves a minister or demonologist in a continuing investigation into where the roots of the haunting began and how to rip them up. This can take weeks, months or sometimes even years. It was by the glory of God that the deliverance took a matter of a few hours. God guided me through it during a time of weakness that I felt. You see I didn't know these people. I didn't know the clients and only met them that night. I never met the paranormal team before and this was the first time I worked with them. I was completely alone representing the church I was a bishop an overseer; and I admit I went into this case with no plans. I completely allowed myself to rely on the guidance of the Holy Spirit. Everything that I did in this case was through Him. All that I did was walk with God, listen, obey and held onto His hand along the way. I don't take any of the credit for being any kind of hero. All that I did was stand in the gap enough to allow God to do His job and deliver the household. I know what you are thinking. "You may have been taken advantage of." This was impossible. The paranormal team that called on me didn't know that I did deliverance ministry, and only thought I was a demonologist who did investigations. No one expected an exorcism to happen and everyone there who witnessed the events that night were taken totally by surprise. There was no way for Lynn to know that I blessed the water she drank that night. Thermo imaging reveals hotter than usual temperatures in Lynn's belly when I placed the Bible on that area. There was no way for Matt to obtain the same name of a spirit in an EVP that was spoken at the house while he was in the store; which was later discovered to be a name for an angel who had authority over black magick.

The Bible tells us that God is love (1 John 4:8). All of us who were involved in this case sacrificed our own needs and desires, moving them away to help a family. This is love. It was love that saved them and love that set them free.

What Kathleen Tedsen and Beverlee Rydel had discovered that in 1870 the antique store was a hardware and general store also used by locals as a center of gossip. The store was rebuilt after a fire that hit the small town that was believed to be caused by an arsonist. The store was owned by Porter A. Wright but the general occupation of the area was farming. The house that the Hay's own use to be owned by W. Philip Stison, and at that time was one of the largest farms in the area. In 1902, Philip's brother Charles and his family decided to leave but his daughter Theresa, who didn't want to leave until she finished school. Philip and his wife Nellie didn't' have any children and agreed to look after Theresa. As Theresa blossomed into a beautiful young woman by age 16, Philip drew notice and they began to flirt and tease one another until they began a relationship that led to incest. Nellie noticed the disgusting advances between the two and expressed her thoughts to Philip who would deny that anything was taking place with his niece. Nellie left the house leaving Theresa at the house with Philip. Two years went by and Theresa had vanished causing locals to ask Philip what happened to her. Philip responded that he wasn't sure until in March of 1904 the gossip of Theresa's whereabouts reached the ears of Porter A. Wright, owner of the general store that is now the antique store in Holly. Porter had received a letter from a sanitarium in Reed City that a young girl died who had been writing a letter on letterhead from Mr. Wright's store. The letter from the sanitarium asked if Mr. Wright had any information on the girl.

Come to find out that Theresa was staying at the sanitarium under an assumed name and Mr. Wright's store was a go between for communication of Philip's and Theresa's secret letters. Theresa died in the sanitarium during child birth and it was believed by locals that the child was the result of Philip's and Theresa's incest. When the town found out Philip was brought up on charges of incest but before they could arrest him he had fled the town. Authorities discovered that Philip was staying in a cabin in a small town in Canada. When authorities arrived to arrest him they overcame him without injury and he was brought back to Holly to await trial.

The trial of Waterman Philip Stison was a Midwest sensation reaching newspapers and filling the courtroom for days. Philip was convicted by damning evidence that Theresa's last words were that Philip was the father of her child. In the end the Michigan Supreme Court overturned the verdict as Philip's lawyer sighted that Theresa's dying words from a secondary source wasn't supporting evidence for the verdict. Philip was free and never returned to the town of Holly again.

It is pain that allows a demon to stack a claim to an area. In such a case as this, it is my expert opinion on demonic legalism that spirits of a sexual nature staked a claim on the old farm. Philip was tempted by a demon that when he acted upon his sexual desires took a claim upon him and everyone in the household. It is difficult to back track upon the demonic claim but I do know that demons will also take civil law; man's made by men, into consideration as well. You see Philip was the head of the household and property owner, so I can only assume that the demon in question entered with the possibility of possessing Theresa to boil the enticements of Philip. When Philip was seduced the demon took spiritual authority. The demon remained in the shadows until something drastic happened to the property. Philip abandoned his land and home causing the demonic forces there to stack a claim. It is my belief that the demons remained there until something triggered them to seek out a new claim.

The irony in this case was that Lynn's uncle sexually abused her and so there was connection between Lynn and Theresa; two women in different timeframes with similar experiences. With Lynn's past experiences allowed the demons in the home to connect to her by similar purposes, and in this case spirit attracted spirit. With her past use of occult practices I believe allowed the demons there to heighten more in their activities. When I was on the case I helped her to regain her legal rights so that the demons there would not be able to hold onto her. In the end they were told to leave and they did rather violently.

However, I do believe that they could return only by the authority of the owners of the land. It doesn't take much for demons to reenter a property they once claimed. Sometimes it only takes a mere word, an invite or just asking for them to show themselves. In any case where there is demonic activity that has been cast out it is important that people do not invited it back in. Just as the great ekballist himself, Jesus once said, "Once a spirit goes out of a man it will walk the earth seeking rest and if it doesn't find any it will return to its original house with seven more demons more powerful than himself." (Luke 11:24)

tHE mount PLEASAnt CREEPER

One late summer's day my wife and I visited a friend of ours at her business. My wife had to stop in and drop off a cake she made for a party. While we were there our friend asked me how deliverance ministry work was going. I replied that things were a little busy but we were managing. She then spoke up and informed us about one of her employees who was having a rather difficult time with a ghost in her new apartment. This employee let our friend know that she needed help and requested for her to set up a meeting with us. She agreed and asked when the soonest we would be available. I mentioned that I was available the coming weekend but liked to keep Sunday's clear for church services.

The same day I received a call from our friend who asked if we could come over to her employee's apartment on Saturday night. I agreed and we had a few talks about how her business was going and her pregnancy. She asked if she could come with us on our visit at her employee's apartment. I informed her that from our experiences with the demonic that they don't like pregnant women and often harass them. She seemed to ignore the danger and insisted on going with us anyway.

When Saturday had come we met in an old Victorian house near downtown Mt. Pleasant. I was amazed at its beauty and couldn't wait to hear more on this case. The house was divided into three separate apartments and rented out to college students who were attending the university. We walked up the stairs to the top apartment and my wife knocked on the door. A woman answered and I asked if Amy was home. She asked us if we were the paranormal investigators and my wife and I looked at each other. We didn't think of ourselves as paranormal investigators. We were mainly from the church community and helped to look into claims from the supernatural. I worked as a deliverance minister and my wife helped me but didn't really have a title or anything. We were just two people with experience in demonic and extreme cases, wanting to help others overcome the devil. My wife and I were quick to respond that we're just there to help.

The young lady, Amy's roommate invited us in. Amy came out and invited us to sit on the couch and let her boss, our friend sit in the lazy boy due to her pregnancy. I asked Amy what was going on and she began to describe how her and her roommate got bored one day and went down in the basement of the house. No one except for the landlord would go down there. There wasn't anything of great interest in the basement so they returned back to their apartment upstairs. After a few days they began to notice odd things happening. In the kitchen a shot glass levitated in the air then fell, and then they noticed the sensation of being groped. More items began to move in the apartment and that was when they decided they needed to seek out help. At times they would run out of the apartment yelling and screaming because a black shadowy figure was creeping across the floor. Amy's boyfriend stayed the night one evening and decided to sleep on the couch when he had seen a shadow in the figure of a person walk around the window blocking out the light from the street. He had gotten up ready to fight an intruder and looked in every room trying to find a thief. Finally the spirit began to talk and sounded like a child. Amy and her roommate gave the spirit they believed was a child the name "Anna."

As the evening turned to night I asked if we could turn the lights off and my wife only had the video camera to see in the dark through night vision. I wanted to see if the apartment was truly haunted, so I asked the spirit to come into the living room area. I rarely ever did this but it was a quick way to see if there was anything in a small area like their apartment. We placed a K2 meter on the coffee table and waited for a short period of time. I then asked Amy to call out Anna. She did and a small sound was heard coming from one of the bedrooms. The two roommates became scared and I quickly got up and went to the room that I thought the bump came from using a flashlight. When I went into Amy's room there was a small doll lying in the middle of the room that wasn't there before while we had a tour of the apartment. I walked in the room and asked if anyone was in there to make a noise. Nothing happened. I walked back to the living area where everyone remained quiet. I stood in the hallway area and asked Amy if she could talk to the spirit for me. I still wasn't convinced that there was a ghost of any kind in their apartment. Amy began to talk to the spirit reminding it of times it did things. I suddenly heard a child's voice in the hallway and the girls asked me if that was me. I replied that it wasn't. Then the dishes in the cupboard moved. I knew then that they had something in their apartment and assumed that if the spirit was able to move objects that it could easily move one of us. I treated the ability of a spirit to move objects as hostile and decided to sit back down in the living room to watch and protect the girls. I knew how to cause harm on a demon with just mere words. All it takes is asking the Holy Spirit to do something to a demon. So I prepared for the worst but I wanted to see if it could do more. There was a large glass container on the coffee table that had a candle in it. I asked the spirit to try and move it and took the video camera from my wife and focused in on the candle. From experience I knew that when a person asked a spirit to do something the spirit would generally not do it but would do something else. I ignored this and felt confident that the spirit would listen and attempt to do it. Suddenly my wife and I's friend felt a hand grab her leg and pull on it. I quickly moved the camera up just in time to get a shot of her leg coming back down. We had warned her that evil spirits would harass her and this one did.

I then treated this spirit as potentially dangerous. I felt that if this haunting were allowed to continue that it would get worse. These were college students and as an ex-college student myself I knew that students never told the whole story. Because of that truth I knew that it was possible that the spirit in question could have come in the apartment through some occult means. It was then that I asked for certain if they ever played with any occult objects. They weren't sure what the occult was so I began listing things like tarot cards and the Ouija board. In the dark of the living room I heard a sadden voice from one of the girls tell me that they did use a Ouija board in the apartment. It was also possible that since it was an apartment that previous tenets may have done something to invite a demon in. I felt the Holy Spirit come over me and tell me to give it a warning. So I did. I spoke up and warned the spirit that if it continued harassing these girls or anyone that walked into the apartment I would hear about it and would cast it out; putting it into a place it wouldn't want to go. I told it to leave and not return in Jesus name. I was prepared for any battle and informed the spirit of the following of ministers I had that would aid me should I need their help. I informed the spirit that there would be ministers filling this apartment casting it into hell if it didn't calm down and leave; that was all I said. I didn't bless the place or anything.

My wife and I got up and Amy turned on the lights. We said our good byes and we all left. Our friend had informed us that she would not be getting into anything that we were doing due to her experience that night with the pulling of her leg. I laughed and told her, "I warned you."

A week later I was driving through Mt. Pleasant and decided to pull into my friend's shop and see if Amy was working. She was and I asked her how things were since our visit. She informed me that nothing was happening in the apartment and everything appeared to be calm. I told her that I was serious in what I told the spirit, that she should contact me right away should something happen. She agreed.

Two weeks went by and I was informed by my friend that the haunting started up again. My friend then informed me that the two roommates had went against my wishes and went back down in the basement, when they had returned to their apartment the spirit followed them and began to haunt their place again. This time I decided not to do anything. There were times when people would bring about things onto themselves and wouldn't listen to me completely ignoring the advice and warnings I would give them. When they ignored me I wouldn't respond to requests for help again. I felt that this time they had truly brought it upon themselves and I felt insulted. I didn't appreciate it when people would think they knew more than me even when I gave them advice from experience and proven two thousand years of Biblical knowledge. I was growing tired of being treated like a butler with clients and began having the attitude that if they can't listen then I can't help. A client's fight is never my fight nor is it God's; it is always the clients fight to free themselves by seeking God out.

After a month of confrontations in their apartment the girls decided to move into a new apartment. In some ways they learnt their lesson and never messed with anything preternatural again. Many of the college students that I helped were secretly performing acts of the occult and were too embarrassed to say anything to me. Nevertheless this case proved to others who heard about it that ekballism can work effectively when used right and with the right words to pluck out an evil spirit.

THE HOUSE ON STEVENSON LAKE ROAD

You never think there is a haunted house near you until someone asks for your help. Sometimes you hear rumors that you think are too far-fetched and are hard to believe. I was rather shocked to learn about this case. The home isn't only ten minutes from my house in Clare, Michigan. Most of the cases I've handled were either in another state, down state, up state and just not near me. This case became so bad that the haunting the family experienced went on for only a week until they had to move out.

Bob Caldwell and his family were moving from Montana to Michigan and were seeking a home to stay in. His sister-n-law's boyfriend had the idea to go in together on renting a home. When they arrived in Michigan they decided to settle on a house south of Clare on Stevenson Lake Rd. One of Bob's friends had purchased the house and informed Bob that he could rent it from him.

The family arrived at the house and turned in the driveway. The moment they pulled in their nine year old twin daughters at the time asked what was in the tree in the front yard. Bob and his wife didn't see anything and asked what they meant by something in the tree. Their daughters said they saw an old woman sitting in the tree that looked like a witch or an old hag. When Bob heard this he felt a little uneasy but didn't think anything of it. He used to be a police officer back in his home state and didn't give the paranormal or supernatural a second thought.

As their first week staying in the house began, their five year old son woke up screaming and claimed that he was woken by what he said was an angel. He described the angel to his father as a bright lady in light wearing a toga of some kind. Bob asked how she woke him up and his son said by blowing on him. He claimed that when the angel spoke to him her voice sounded like music. The next night the angel woke him up again and asked him to follow her down stairs. He followed and saw what he described as a blue tornado in front of the dining area near his parents door. The angel asked him to enter the blue twister but he said he only peeked inside. When Bob asked him what he saw his son described that the inside of the tornado had hundreds of workers. When he pulled his head back he could see thousands of angels in the house and even hovering over his parents. Bob was a little disturbed by his son's story until his daughters told him that they woke up one night to see their brother standing in the hall way standing still for what seemed to be five minutes. Bob then decided that he needed to contact someone and found John and Karen Mealer in Clare of Central Michigan Paranormal Investigations.

Bob talked with the Mealers in private and informed them of what his family had already experienced. The Mealers informed Bob they wouldn't be able to get out to the house right way but would try. When Bob hung up the phone his son asked him when the camera people were coming over. Bob asked what camera he was referring to and his son told him that the angel told him that there would be people over soon who would take pictures of them. Bob was shocked as he was alone when he talked with John and Karen His curiosity about the home began to grow even more. He now knew that something was very wrong about the home and was concerned for his family. Bob knew that there was no way for his son to know that John and Karen were coming over, and that experience alone sent chills up his spine.

Before the Mealers would arrive the angel people in the home began to become more hostile to the family. Everywhere Bob's wife walked in the home a clawing sound on the walls would follow her. Bob knew it wasn't mice in the walls because the sound was more of a dragging, sounded like finger nails on the walls and only happened around his wife. His wife took a digital camera and began taking pictures to discover bright lights and fog near them on the digital camera monitor. In the middle of the day the washer and dryer were not in use and sounded like someone was beating them violently. Their dog spotted something and its back hair stood up as it starred at midair. The dog then tried to wedge itself between the couch and the wall and began vomiting.

The next night Bob woke up to find his son standing in his doorway starring out of his bedroom. He got out of bed and asked his son if he was alright and his son asked him if he saw her. "Who?" Bob asked. "The little girl." He responded. "She has duct tape over her mouth." Bob quickly turned the lights on and his son told him that she disappeared when the lights came on.

Finally the Mealers were able to perform an investigation into the home. The team was made up of two women and three men. The Mealers asked Bob and his wife to investigate with them so that they could help to identify what the family was seeing. The women went upstairs while the men went in the basement. While upstairs the women claimed to hear clawing on the walls and growling. In the basement one of the investigators named Gabe DeLeon asked if anyone was there to make a sound. As soon as he asked there was a bang above them. Investigators John Mealer and John Smith then sighted a black shadow figure and when they got up stairs they spotted the baby gate in the middle of the floor that was far from where it should be. That alone was enough for Bob and his wife, as they left half way through the investigation and didn't return to the house.

After the investigation John Mealer had went through the material they obtained and discovered an EVP from a spirit telling Bob's son to hide. Bob's son wasn't at the investigation at the time. The children were sent away to a friend's house while Bob and his wife assisted the Mealers and their team. John had also obtained a mysterious EVP of a name that they couldn't place. When Bob was doing research on the house later he could attribute the name to the house.

John called me and asked me to come over to the house the following night and I agreed. He wanted me to investigate the house with him and spot anything demonic. I didn't think much would happen while I was on the second investigation. Demons seemed to hide from me at the time and I've been on many investigations where there were a lot of extreme claims but when I showed up nothing would happen. Sure enough when I arrived and explored the house at night, I went upstairs and didn't experience anything. I waited it out with Gabe in the boy's bedroom even getting toys out of Bob's son's toy box to make the spirit feel as if the boy were there. However, I had heard and seen the evidence that the Mealers and their team obtained except for one of the EVP's. From what I heard from the EVP's and the photo and video evidence I made the determination that it was demonic. Like many cases before, these demons also hid from my presence. Experts say that when demons do this they are afraid of a confrontation with God. I wasn't sure about that. I was just a man of God who obeyed and did what the Holy Spirit told me to do. At this time, no matter how boring it may have been, He told me to just show up.

After the second investigation John informed Bob that I would do a binding on the home that would last enough to allow them to get in and get their things to move out. A binding was the best I could do since the house was a rental. I could not perform a blessing or an exorcism on the home because Bob didn't own it. Doing a blessing or exorcism would be like trespassing, so I believed that a binding would hold back or calm down the spirits in the home long enough for Bob and his family to move out.

The next day I grabbed my bag of tricks and drove back over to the house on Stevenson Lake Road. I pulled in with John while Bob let us in. Bob left telling us that him and his family didn't want to be around the house while we were there doing the binding. I walked in and sat my things on the table. It was quiet as John watched me gather up holy water from the bag and poured it into a holy water sprinkler. I grabbed extra holy water in case something happened or ran out in the sprinkler. I had blessed salt with me also as that would act as a long lasting blessing. Salt didn't evaporate like water did. Salt is stone and doesn't go away. So even if the demons came back the salt alone would frustrate and torment them.

I began in the basement and placed blessed salt everywhere. I said a prayer of protection and began the binding. I threw holy water in all four corners and demanded the demons to either show themselves or leave in Jesus name. Nothing happened. If there were a demon he would manifest himself in some way through a heaviness or lightheadedness, maybe even a black mass or an audible voice. If that happened then John and I would have to deal with the demons right there and possibly do battle against them. I hope it wouldn't have to come to that. I was hoping that the demons would get startled and just leave the house or hide until Bob's family left.

In this seemingly piece of American farm country, while farmers used their tractors, cars drove by and farm animals were feeding, we were in a small home binding demons. In a way I was reminded of that old saying, "In outer space no one can hear you scream." If these demons decided to show themselves, no one would know we were there in farm country. John and I were alone in the house and would have to fend off the attacks should something wicked and come our way.

After binding the basement I made my way into each room performing the binding until I made it to the hallway upstairs passing portraits of Bob's family. I went into each room performing the binding, staying quiet after speaking the words that would determine whether or not a demon would leave or show itself. We would stop and listen for any noise, voices or sign of demonic activity then continue. I informed John that anything could still happen so we quietly made our way back downstairs where we heard a bump. We paused for a moment to watch the house. I looked outside and noticed the wind was blowing and contributed the bump to something hitting the house outside but John said he thought it came from inside. We gave the binding time and I yelled aloud so every room in the house could hear me. "If there is anyone here I demand you make a noise now or leave in Jesus name!" We paused to listen and pay attention to our surroundings. I felt my discernment reach every corner of the home to feel any sense of a demonic presence but I couldn't find any. John and I looked at each other and we were certain that the binding worked. We gathered up are equipment and left out the kitchen door. I stopped John and prayed over us that no spirits from the house and property would attach themselves to us. As we reached out cars I looked back at the house and was in wonder over what could have taken place there in the past to cause such a frightful haunting.

A few years hand went by and I had contacted Bob to talk with him about the house on Stevenson Lake Road more. A lot of the events in this story I was unaware had taken place at the time. I relied on my friends John & Karen Mealer, John Smith and Gabe DeLeon that I trusted and personally taught demonology to. I trusted their testimonies on the house and believed the evidence they gathered.

As I talked with Bob he had informed me that he put his police skills to work. Bob use to be a police officer and didn't believe much of the paranormal. He was a man who used to take criminals down and arrest them and he was a man who didn't get scared easily. Bob informed me that he had never been more scared in his life while living in that house. He told me how he went to the local library and looked through old newspapers and did his own research on the house. I was curious as to what he discovered and pressed the phone closer to my ear. Bob had discovered that in 1978 a murder took place in the house. A story of wife kills her husband. I knew the story behind this while I went on John's second investigation. I recalled Bob telling John about the murder and John pointing at the floor boards upstairs of where Bob said the murder took place. Such a murder would solidify a demons claim to the area that caused the wife to murder her husband. But Bob told me something that got deep down in my soul. What he told me next was about an EVP that John got at the house that he never shared with me. Unknown to Bob and John the EVP was a direct message from the devil to me. At the time of this case I was looking for my old high school sweetheart so I could apologize to her on how I treated her in the past. I had no intensions of committing any adultery, I was in a sense on an apology tour trying to contact all the people in my past that I hurt or offended; to clear my conscience and have a better state of mind. Bob told me that the EVP that John obtained at the house was of a name that he couldn't place with the house. He told me the name and my mouth dropped. The name was of my high school sweetheart. I informed him of this and Bob was shocked as well. We ended our conversation and I moved myself over to my sliding glass door and look out to the woods beyond my pond. It was then that I realized that I needed to pay more attention on every case I go on. I knew the devil watched me but I didn't realize that he was watching me that close. I looked back at all the cases that followed the Stevenson Lake Road House and the answer to my question on why things were getting harder for me was answered by a single EVP that I never heard. If I had heard the EVP before I probably would have prepared myself for what was coming.

†HE DEMONIC NETWORK

In 2010 I agreed to look into a case of demonic possession that I will never forget. Matt Moyer obtained a case of demonic possession and gave it me to look into. It would also be my first unsuccessful attempt at casting out demons. However, I witnessed something that helped to prove that there is a demonic network of communication. The theory in demonology research and deliverance ministry is that demons have the ability to teleport across thousands of miles in the blink of an eye, and can call for assistance at a moment's notice.

As a woman who claimed to be possessed traveled to meet me our church booked a room for her and her boyfriend at a local hotel. I know what you are thinking. What is a church doing booking a room for a woman and her boyfriend when they are not married? Well, for one I don't condone any sex before marriage nor living together before wedlock, however her and her boyfriend were of upper middle age. They were respectful adults who honored my request to not have any relations while in the room. Also, she was a woman that was suffering a great deal from demonic possession and needed company while on her trip to Michigan. Her son lived in another state and wasn't able to be with her through the process. So as a deliverance minister I was glad to see her boyfriend was with her through it all.

At this moment in my life performing deliverance ministry I became prideful and believed that God would help me cast out any demon anywhere. I admit at that point I wasn't taking the time to listen to God like I should have in so many successful cases before. I did feel that God was telling me that these demons wanted me and not the client. I was in for a whole new experience, not knowing I was positioning myself for a trap.

It seemed that the devil and I were playing a game while my ministry was at full throttle. It felt like wherever I went evil spirits wouldn't reveal themselves, and people plagued with possession would report that there weren't any problems after I just visited. Cases felt as if all I had to do was show up and sit in a chair to talk with a client, maybe at times see a few acts of demonic activity, counsel and leave and nothing more would happen. The deliverance ministry wasn't a challenge for me anymore and was becoming too easy. It was as if demons were afraid of me. I'd show up on a case, leave and nothing more would happen. I almost felt as if the devil was bored with me now. In some ways because of the lack of resistance on their end I felt prideful, superior over evil spirits and my ego rose too far. My wife even tried to bring me down a few notches being a critic at my every move in sermons and church operations. However, I felt this kind of resistance from friends and my wife was normal but it actually wasn't. I felt that because of the lack of demonic counter attacks and weak resistance that I had finally achieved the type of deliverance ministry I dreamed about. I was finally performing an ekballistic ministry. Where ever I went demons were being plucked out left and right. My ministry was like a steamroller over the works of the devil until this case taught me a thing or two.

As the woman was on her way I received a phone call from my friend Tracy Bacon who is a demonologist from Indiana. We were talking about his interesting case of a stage five haunting that became dangerous in Indiana. Together we tried to figure out the root source of how the entity got into the home. I mentioned to him that pastors will sometimes use a possessed person for interrogation to find out information on other cases. It is equal to capturing a spy and interrogating them on the enemy defenses. Tracy was willing to try it and drove up with a friend to help with the deliverance of the woman. A local pastor and good friend from a church close to us allowed me to use his churches basement for the deliverance. The woman's case was so extreme that I asked people with CPR experience to attend and asked Lynn Hay who had now received a level of discernment from her possession after the Holly case. Lynn was able to now see spirits and I felt that I could help her tune these skills to help her. All these people agreed to help. I even asked a few strong people to help with holding the woman down should these demons seek to attack me. I felt in my spirit that this case was going to be a hard one but was confident that God would not forsake me.

The woman arrived at the hotel room and was checked in. My friend John Mealer, who was also a demonologist, assisted me in helping her settle in her room. As we entered the room we greeted her and her boyfriend and sat down to talk. She filled out some paperwork from our church, and then I received a phone call and took it outside. It was Tracy who informed me that he and his friend had arrived at my house and was there with my wife. I informed him that I would be there shortly as John and I were helping the woman to settle in. When I arrived back at the room John was still conversing with the couple. I proceeded to ask the woman about the demons and if she could feel them now. She mentioned that they were pressing on her head. I took a Gideon Bible out of a drawer in the room and placed it by her. She was quick to notice that the Bible was near her. At times during the conversation she would look down at the Bible as if it were a thorn in her side. I began to teach here about how demons enter a person to find out the root cause of her possession when John spoke up and asked me a question. "Do demons have sexes?" The next thing we knew the Gideon Bible flew across the room and a different voice come out of the woman. "Of course we have sexes!" All eyes in the room were quickly on the woman and it became quiet. I was shocked at how quickly the demon came out. I was used to being comfortable in avoiding the intelligence of a demon at this time because they seemed like they were avoiding me. I was the first to speak asking who was speaking. "Wouldn't you like to know." was the response I got. I asked again who was speaking and all I got in return was a sinister grin. John asked me if he could ask the demon a question and I agreed figuring that he needed to know how these things operated since he was new at the time. He asked the demon if they did have genders and the demon replied that they did. It was at this time that I realized that if this was a sensitive subject for demons then it could be used against them to discover where they may be hiding on cases.

Since John was a newer demonologist at the time and an apprentice I allowed him to converse with the demon. In the training I gave him I reminded him that whatever demons speak to you treat it as a lie. I also taught him from experience that demons will only pay attention to whoever speaks to them. In this case I notice the woman's composure was that of only talking to whoever spoke to her. Psychologically women can handle multiple conversations at once, even listening to a conversation next to them while talking to one person. Mothers have the ability to listen to both children while they argue. Men on the other hand can't handle more than one conversation at a time. Men become upset when two or more people are talking to them. This was a different situation. When the woman came forward she could listen to all of us in the room even hear the people in the other neighboring rooms. But when this entity came forward it only would listen to one person at a time. This told me that we were talking with a male entity.

The woman's widened eyes were only trained on me and she avoided the other men in the room until John asked the demon a few questions, they answered and I began to laugh. The woman quickly turned to me staring. "Why do you think it is funny!" it responded. "Because I know you're giving him b.s.", I said. The demon through the woman just gave me a straight faced look. I told the demon, "O.k. you have free rein to say what you want in this moment in time. Go ahead and tell us where demons come from." I said this to help in John's training to help him understand the lies that demons tell. I quickly thought of Lilith, the Demon Queen who was believed by Satanists to be the first wife of Adam. The demon responded to my question with, "We come from Lilith." I laughed again and the demon asked me why I was laughing. I responded that I knew it was b.s. They responded that she was in the tree when it happened. I wasn't sure what "when it happened" meant. However, I have to admit that I told the demon to answer the question because I was thinking about Lilith. I knew the possession that the woman was facing was purely genuine because it read my thoughts.

I knew the Lilith legend so well and the interesting thing was I was studying Lilith at the time. I began to believe that demon knew that I was studying Lilith and decided to push me into wanting to believe the lie, however I knew better. It was at this moment that I knew that I was dealing with what I called a "master mind". I call these demons this because of how well they can mess with you. They have an objective and they are very smart. They are the type of demons that are the sinister villain in a mystery novel. The villain in the novel has an objective that the hero is trying to figure out. Before the hero can figure out the villain's goal their plan is already in motion. With these demons you don't know what they are up to.

I was too anxious to know what was happening in Tracy's case that I jumped the gun and asked the demons about Tracy's case in Indiana. The demon responded that it was big. I asked the Holy Spirit to cause torment on the demon should it lie to me. The demon wouldn't give me any more information. I tried again but it refused to speak about the entity in that case.

I had to try and get the information out the best I could so I thought of ways that I could try and out maneuver the demon and catch it off its guard. I knew that demons were prideful so I asked it about itself. And it told me that there were three spirits in the woman. I asked where he thought he was and he said that he was to the woman's right near the lamp. I asked where the others were and it gave me the run around that they weren't here right now. I quickly had a thought that I wondered if they left to visit the case in Indiana I mentioned to it. I stood there and waited while the demon through the woman starred at me wide eyed. For a moment it was as if two master minds were trying to out maneuver each other. It was quiet for a moment then John spoke up and asked how many demons where in the woman again. One of the demons spoke up and said we are now four. I was now growing worried that my pride got in the way by jumping the gun and starting the interrogation to early. I felt that the demon that was haunting the home in Indiana was now with us also in the hotel room. "Who is the new spirit that is with us now?" I asked trying to find some footing to outwit the demons. She looked at me away from John and responded, "That is none of your concern."

After a short struggle I made the demons in the woman to go down and forbid them from harming her so she could get a good night's sleep. I dropped John off at his house. John informed me that he felt that these were big ones. I told him that I believed they were as well. He walked in his house and I backed up and drove home. I was a little worried that these powerful demons may have followed me home. Thoughts entered my mind of my car crashing into a tree or a possessed driver of a truck would hit me. I felt like I was being chased or followed in some way. There is no telling what these type of demons can do. They can possess a person, make them kill someone and leave and before you know it you see dead people and the police are taking you away for murder. They are masterminds or what the Bible calls in Ephesians chapter six, "powers." I headed for home to greet Tracy and his friend. We stayed up talking for a short period and my wife prepared the guest bedroom for them to sleep in and we all retired for the night. I could hardly sleep. I kept thinking what if these masterminds are in my home right now and I didn't know it. What if they were going to kill us in the middle of the night? I've faced many demons before but I knew these ones were up to something. Something sinister and I knew they had a plan. I decided to not change anything in the deliverance the next day and just move as planned.

In the morning my wife made us all breakfast when Tracy and his friend sat down to eat and mentioned about leaving to go home. I asked why and they informed me that they received a phone call at 2 a.m. from their case in Indiana that all hell had broken loose last night. I was shocked, I asked why they were leaving and they mentioned that objects were coming alive and a dresser was walking out of a room on its own. I mentioned then to them of what I had asked the demons out of the woman. I had interrogated the demons early and jumped the gun. We were all shocked at the turn of events and Tracy and his friend were concerned that they were too far for them to drive back to help. I assured them that we needed to press on and interrogate these demons to obtain more information for their case. They decided to go through with it.

Tracy and his friend followed us to the church my pastor friend had allowed us to do the deliverance in. Our church was between buildings at the time so we needed a location to help this woman. I would have gladly done it out of our home but my wife was always against the idea of performing deliverance in our house. I had too much of a warm heart for people wanting to help them that I would give my shirt off my back. She didn't understand what it was like to be a victim of a possession. However, I did and a person who becomes possessed is desperate for help.

When we arrived at the church I unlocked the door and entered. I quickly went in the basement in the prayer room and set things up. Tracy, his friend and my wife all followed. I left to wait for the others to come who would assist me. My wife and I had a plan. We would use the room next door to the prayer room as a place for all the prayer warriors who were going to pray and we wouldn't tell the woman.

People began to arrive and we began telling people our plan however their curiosity was getting the best of them and they all said they wanted to watch. I couldn't lose the much needed prayer that was needed for the deliverance so I kindly asked again for prayer warriors to follow my wife into the room next door. But some of the people felt that their drive justified them to watch instead of pray. I was angry at this type of behavior coming out of the people who were part of my ministry. I threw my hands up and walked away.

The morning was sunny however as we all stood there talking waiting for the woman and her boyfriend to arrive it began to rain. Finally they had arrived at the church and a member of my team opened the door for them and let them in. I introduced the couple to my teammates and why they were there. I had two people with me who were certified with CPA training, two demonologists, Lynn for discernment, a paranormal investigator and a prayer warrior who I actually needed for his strength.

While I was out in the hallway getting my things ready John had taken me off to the side and asked me if I experienced anything odd last night. I informed him that I did not but didn't mention what happen in Indiana. He told me that he received a weird phone call that his caller i.d. displayed as "unavailable". He answered it to discover someone breathing on the other end. He asked who was there then heard a man's voice say "Shut up!" I kind of blew it off as nothing but kept it in the back of my mind.

When I reentered the room to bring in more tools for the deliverance I looked through the small basement window and noticed the sun was shining. I looked down at the woman and took a seat in the middle of the room in front of her. James, our prayer warrior took a seat next to the woman to my right while Tracy sat next to her on my left. John sat in a chair next to me against the window. Two women, one sat behind me. I needed Lynn who has discernment to sit behind me in case I couldn't spot something supernatural.

My first objective was to spiritually heal the woman. I needed her to talk with me about the abuse she received. She agreed and as she talked I began to ask her to repeat an oath for me. The oath was for her to renounce the abuse. As she was trying to renounce the abuse she received I glanced up in the small window and noticed that it was raining outside. I looked back down at the woman to see her staring at me. I knew then the demons came forward. They mentioned how they didn't like what I was doing. I would command them to go down and bring the woman back up. This was an endless cycle having the woman come up in consciousness, say a few words of renouncing things then the demons in her would come up to put a pause on everything. This was frustrating. Having her renounce things was like listening to a song on a CD and listening to it skip. At times I felt like my rhythm was off. I devised a new strategy by trying to turn the lower demons against the higher one. I commanded the lowest demon to come up and he did. I began to talk to him about the others in the woman. I asked him if he felt belittled by them and he agreed. I asked him if he was tired of being used by the higher one. He replied that he was getting tired of his energy being used. I asked him if he hated the highest in the woman and he said that he did. I told him that he should come against him. "I'd like to." He replied. What I was doing was trying to use the devil's own technique of divide and counter against him. It worked. It gave me time to call the woman back up while the demons fought amongst each other. The woman was able to renounce things which gave me time until the demons finally appeared to get things under control. "Think you're smart don't you!" One of them told me. I began to laugh and began to interrogate the demons on the case in Indiana. Again, one of them said he, in referring to the demon in Indiana was big. I commanded the demon to tell me more and how the demon got in the home. He refused, so I asked the Holy Spirit to cause torment on him in Jesus name. He acted as if he suddenly received pain and became angry at me. I told him to answer my question truthfully or I'll ask the Holy Spirit to torment him again. He growled through the woman and began speaking another language. If he answered me in another language that I was unfamiliar with he had me at a disadvantage. I only knew a little Hebrew and some Greek. When he spoke I was able to understand the dialect enough to know that the bastard was replying to me in another language. To make sure I said, "Boker Tov" which in Hebrew means, "Good Morning" or "Good Day". He replied with a speedy Hebrew but what I could make out was that something would happen that day. I replied and demanded only English be spoken and to answer my questions in English. Again the reply was in a different language and I asked the Holy Spirit to cause torment upon the demons in Jesus name. Again they appeared to be in pain. They then looked at me intently through the woman. In a split second I decided to ask God to myself to make angels present to put pressure on the demons in accordance with John 14:14. Suddenly I saw the woman look around the room and at the ceiling. "What did you do?" they asked me. I didn't reply.

This struggle with went on for the first three hours to try and obtain any information and to find out how the demons got in the woman. The whole process felt like two rams locked at the horns pushing each other back and forth. Finally I decided we had just enough information to determine that the demons entered in a fashion relating to the abuse she had received. I could tell that she had trouble trying to forgive the men who abused her, and I knew that if she couldn't completely forgive them that she was a lost cause. I knew I would lose this one because it wasn't my fight nor was it God's fight. The fight was in the hands of the woman. It was up to her to whole heartedly request God to step in and deliver her. So I decided to send the devil a message and he would receive it well; enough for him to make a personal appearance.

The demons began to speak in other languages again. I felt the Holy Spirit tell me to call my friends Noah and have the Demons speak to him and find out what they were saying. Noah was a paranormal investigator out of Southern Ohio that I met while I investigated Bobby Mackey's. We became quick friends and we connected through Jewish culture and his roots. Oddly enough I grabbed my cell phone and dialed him. I got his voice mail and asked Noah to translate the following... I took my phone and put it up to the woman's ear and told the demons to speak Hebrew. One of them muttered something in the phone. I left a message and hung up. Then got out my binder with the oath of exorcism and proceeded to command the demons to repeat after me. They said they wouldn't and so I caused torment on them again to remind them of God's power. They screamed in pain and I could see some kind of supernatural force take hold of them. I again told the demons to repeat after me. Prior to this I had obtained two of the demons names, so I began with the highest one to say an oath before God of its own banishment. My message to the devil began.

The struggle was tiring and the woman and I were both getting tired. I was only able to get the demons to say half of the oath and then they didn't want to play anymore. They mysteriously left but they didn't leave the presence of the woman. After her deliverance she was still suffering periods of possession. I knew I'd lose, not because of the strength of these powers but because of the will of the woman was weak. She would need months or maybe even years of counseling from a pastor to build her strength before a full on deliverance could take place. She would have to want them out but by the manner of her diameter I knew she was holding onto something the demons provided that she liked. I wasn't sure what it was and if I did I'd find some way to use it against them to free the woman.

She would need to be with a congregation and a pastor in her area in her state. I sat down with her again and counseled her on what she needed to do. She was heartbroken and I felt for her suffering but she needed to take instruction in order to be free. She wanted to find an exorcist who could cast out the demons like the wave of a magic wand. *Magic wand*, was a term I always heard from people. "You don't have like a magic wand and just make them leave?" The devil didn't work that way. He is like a prosecuting attorney always accusing humanity and taking rights away from us. His demons had a right to be in her but I wasn't sure what those rights were. To many times I saw this in my ministry and was why I sent the devil a personal message. You see, the devil knew I knew I was going to lose. I knew that he knew that without finding the rights I couldn't do anything. So my message to the devil was doing the exorcism anyway and through it symbolically telling him, "I'm not taking your crap anymore." About a quarter the way through the oath of exorcism the woman's voice and eyes changed. A new voice and face came through that looked at me and said, "Why do you fight me? You always have to fight me." The Holy Spirit spoke up inside me and told me that this was the devil in person talking to me. I responded to him; "I will always fight you." Then I continue with the rest of the oath of exorcism. Tracy and James and I had trouble restraining the woman at times and at one point she actually picked all three of us up at the same time. These demons were more resistant than anything I handled before that it literally felt like putting a steal rod in a position to gain leverage and trying to bend it. At first it appears that the steel rod won't bend but the more pressure you put upon it the more it gives but there is still a resistance in it. Just as you think you have enough leverage on the bar the bar springs back into its original position. It was frustrating and the most intense spiritual warfare I've ever experienced.

Later in the day I received a call from Noah who interpreted the Hebrew the woman spoke. He said that the language spoken was actually Aramaic and that she said, "I challenge the guardian, the guardian cannot." Noah then hung up and I noticed my phone had instantly shut off. I would have problems with my phone turning on and shutting off for a week until it got back to normal. The shocking thing was that my name in Latin means, "Guardian". I knew that these demons were directly challenging me. However, the most interesting thing was the year that followed. Almost overnight the congregation in the church that the deliverance was performed in began to come against the senior pastor in secret. The church election for the senior pastor came and half of the congregation wanted him while the other half did not. The senior pastor was able to stay on as pastor of the church by one vote. The youth pastor mysteriously left the church and town. It was later discovered that the reason why he left was due to performing sexual sins. The senior pastor later left due to a small stroke. However, the Lord did restore the church with new pastors who healed the congregation.

This story goes to show how dangerous messing with the demonic is. These powers, these masterminds had a plan and fulfilled it. I believe their plan was to destroy me and to destroy a church. Since this case I suffered through a period of misfortunate.

Around a few weeks later I traveled down to Indiana with Tracy, John and an apprentice to help him with his case. We drove twelve hours straight and when we got there we investigated the home. I heard the EVP's, saw the photos and video but still wanted it to be proven to me. That night we set up a K2 grid in the living room and Tracy used a trifield meter to confirm any hits from the K2's. It was the most interesting demonic activity I ever seen. We could see the demon walk in the living room and out and each K2 would light up one at a time. This happened all night and even when we went to bed. I awoke from my sleep to feel a type of static electricity near my face. I turned my head slowly to see if there was a shadow over me and spotted Tracy on the floor watching a K2 near me in the red. When I turned my head to see the K2 and moved my body I could feel the static on me. Each time I would move my body just a little bit the K2 would go into the red. After a few minutes the static finally went away and the K2 lights went down and then off.

We never could establish or understand what the rights were that granted these powers to be in the home. The case was similar to an invisible man walking through the house. The residence claimed that the demon would speak audibly to them but I personally never experienced this. The demon would perform its period of torments on the family seasonally. The family would experience periods of peace in their home but when a holiday such as Christmas, Easter and the period of Lent all hell would break loose in the home.

Sadly, these cases forced me to move away from them in the end. If the rights were discovered something could be done to remove these powers from their grip on these people. The other reason that we couldn't do anything was the lack on the clients end to do what we asked them to do. I was never asked to perform an exorcism on the house in Indiana and the woman who I performed deliverance on never did any of the instructions I requested that would put her on the path to allow God to deliver her. In a sense these two cases were a major battlefield on both ends of the spectrum. Neither side won but the battles were spiritually bloody and weakening. After the woman's six hour deliverance I was dripping in sweat and John spoke up to me and said, "I could feel the tension in the atmosphere of the room."

tHE ALMA PRINCIPALITY

I held a lecture on demonology and deliverance in the autumn of 2010 and asked several friends to speak with me. My concern was that paranormal investigators would get hurt if they dealt with possible demonic cases. I've had friends in the paranormal field that either got possessed, scratched or hit by demons just by trying to find out what were in homes. So I decided to help educate people who wanted to know more about demons. Several people bought tickets and showed up to listen to us speak. It was an all-day event with a dinner at the end. Several of the guests appreciated the lecture and those who couldn't come asked that I would have another one. The problem was money issues otherwise I would have continued having lectures and travel to take it to other states in the Mid-West.

I had informed several of the guests that if they had a case that they felt was too difficult for them that they could pass it onto me as long as they had evidence to support that it was demonic. Many of them agreed except for the wiccans who showed up and argued with one of the speakers while he spoke and me later. We held our ground though because my friend who spoke, Randy Ervin and I were Christians and only spoke from what the Bible says about evil spirits. The wiccan argument that their religion is older than Christianity didn't hold ground. As occult experts we knew that Gerald Gardner founded the religion in the early twentieth century and was a disciple of Alistair Crowley, the famous founder of modern day Satanism. The

Christian Church has over two thousand years of experience dealing with evil spirits with a success record of casting them out unmatched by any other religion.

I fully expected at least a few of the paranormal investigators who showed up to call me, and in about a month one did. Bob, who was an independent investigator, received two different cases out of the Alma, Michigan area. One was of a demonic spirit who was plaguing a handicap woman with a mental disorder. Bob did everything right in that case for me. He knew I would try and push it off as part of her mental disorder and he got through the objective diagnosis I have on each case that crosses my desk. He obtained evidence to support the woman's claim that something was plaguing her and her granddaughter. I agreed to drive over and perform a cleansing of the home with holy incense. The woman wasn't possessed in any way. She was only be harassed by something in her home that she couldn't see.

I met Bob at the local McDonald's and I followed him over to the lady's home. When we arrived he went in and informed her that I was there to perform a cleansing. Bob then motioned for me to come in. Upon entering I was greeted by a woman in a wheel chair who was very kind. Bob stayed in the living room while I talked with the woman in her kitchen. She had informed me of the various things that the entity would do to her. At night the spirit would try to have sex with her by feeling her up and trying to penetrate her. When I heard this I knew I was dealing with an incubus, an evil spirit of sexual nature that preyed on lust. These spirits were bullies to woman and it just made me righteously angry that this spirit was doing such things to a handicap woman. She took me on a tour of her house showing me all the places where attacks strung up. Most of the attacks were in the bathroom. The spirit would make faces in the foggy mirror, write on the floor with lip stick and ugly faces would appear through the walls. The spirit wouldn't stop there. Foul odors would fill the house like rotten eggs and sulfur. I instantly asked Bob if the plumbing was checked and he mentioned that since it was city connected he spoke with the neighbors to see if they were having problems which they weren't. Bob also checked her plumbing in which everything appeared to be fine. I asked if she had a garbage disposal and she replied that she did not. After a long conversation to help her feel at ease over what she had been facing and building her faith, I proceeded to burn the gloria incense I had in my Orthodox incense burner. I went through the house without any resistance while Bob followed me with his recorder. We were done, and I bid the lady good night and left with Bob. Bob agreed to monitor her case which he did for months and the attacks on her stopped the day since the cleansing.

While I waited for any other cases to come in I received case after case from the Alma area. One group informed me of a home they investigated in Alma where a family used a Ouija board and started getting activity in their home. The group informed the family of me and they replied that they wanted the activity and declined the offer to have the spirits cast out. I always thought it was odd that home owners actually wanted the activity in their home and thought it was cool.

The same group received a claim for another Alma family that a grandmother and her granddaughters were being plagued by moving objects. Nothing was done in this case when the group asked the family if they wanted me to come in and cast the spirits out. The old lady decided she had enough retirement money to just move out. I never heard anything back on that claim.

Bob called me later and needed help with a demonic case in yet Alma again. I replied to him, wondering why there were so many cases coming out of Alma. I assume that a principality was involved. A principality is a governing spirit over other spirits in a general area. If someone was to play with a Ouija board for example and continually mess with it, it is possible that the haunting would spread to the neighbors. If more occult media were used then the haunting could spread to a whole block and then onto the next until an entire city was taken over by demonic forces. They are not hard to spot. All that a person would have to do is watch the news to see the amount of murders, thefts, rapes and crime increases in one single area over a period of time. The demonic spirits in the area entice people to do things and act unnatural. Businesses mysteriously close down and illness rises in the area. A good example of a principality is the city of Detroit, Michigan. Detroit has an issue with gang related activity, rape and murder. Sometimes the history of an area has a pressing point upon a community. If there were Native American battles during colonial times in an area there is a good chance that the spirits that influenced the murders during the battle would stay in the area to influence future generations. A deliverance minister or demonologist would have a very hard time taking on a principality on their own. I would never recommend anyone taking on a principality. The only real way that a principality can be cast out of an area is by the evangelism of a church or churches. That is just what I did. Before this principality had the chance to even begin to influence the Alma community I proceeded to inform Pastor Bill about it who gladly brought in his troops and evangelized the area. They blew their shofars and talked with people converting them to Christ. Bill and his troops informed me of a mass revealing of demons coming out of people as they talked with them on the streets.

Bill and I fooled the devil sort of speak. While he and his Christian troops were evangelizing on the streets of downtown Alma I was working on a case given to me by Bob. I figured that by Bill keeping the devil worried of a Christian invasion sort of speak of the city I could better help a mother and daughter.

Bob's case was very interesting to me. Bob obtained evidence of moving objects and audible voices. The demon in the home was causing so much fear from the mother and daughter that once something moved they would pack up their things and stay the night with the grandmother. I agreed to pay the mother and daughter a visit. I arrived at night and followed Bob over. I brought my wife and a new apprentice Sally with me who left the occult behind to live a life for Christ. Sally wanted to become a demonologist/exorcist and I agreed to take her under my wing and show her the ropes of deliverance ministry. We were invited in and I quickly noticed how clean the home was which I thought was unusual since most of the demonic hauntings

I handled had a hint of carelessness. Bob talked with the mother and daughter for some time while I listened. I generally studied people's body language and could tell when someone was telling a lie or telling the truth. If their palms were out and open then they were telling the truth but when the palms were down I knew they were lying. There were other methods I could tell when someone was lying. I studied psychology and neuro-linguistic programming (NLP) which helped a lot to understand what people were really thinking. I was very interested in mentalism and learned to apply it to demonology investigations. I was experiencing a mass amount of demonic claims and got tired of driving far distances only to find out that the case were a fraud. So I defended myself with psychology and NLP which helped also to understand when someone was actually possessed or not or playing around with me.

After talking with the mother for some time I wanted to learn about their case for myself. I let the mother tell me the story and what was happening. Sure enough Bob was right. When something moved they would run out of the house and drive down to the grandmother's house. I had my questioning down to a fine tune like a five string guitar knowing what sounds made the right note. I knew what questions to ask that would reveal a true possession. For me it got to the point where I only have to ask just two questions. Have you ever been sexually abuse? And, have you ever practiced the occult? The combination of those two together was deadly which initiated instant possession. My form of questioning also helped me to determine whether or not a case was fake. Several times I caught people performing fraud just by questioning them, and each time I was slandered by those same people not for authenticating their case. I wasn't about to put my name on a case unless there was undeniable evidence to support the claim.

My team and I spoke with the mother and daughter in their home for several hours. I asked the mother if her ex-husband had ever abused her. She replied that he had. I then asked if either one of them had performed any media of the occult. They asked me to expand my question so I gave examples such as tarot cards, black magic, spells or a Ouija board. I noticed that the daughter had widened her eyes when I said Ouija board so I called her out on it by asking her how long she had been using the board. She appeared shocked that I knew. I asked who the spirit was that came through the board. The daughter replied that it was a boy from school who passed away. I wanted to inform the mother and daughter the dangers of playing with a Ouija board but I decided against it so I could obtain more information on the evil spirit that was plaguing them. I wanted to know how it was playing out its part in the haunting and where it was. With all the experience I had running through my head I felt that the spirit was in or near the mother due to her abuse she received from her ex-husband. So I looked at her and ask how long she was hearing the spirit. Her eyes widened and she gasped. She placed her hand to her mouth and looked down. I looked at her daughter and she seemed to be interested in knowing what was going on. Bob appeared to be amazed at the way I was finding things out. The atmosphere in the home began to feel tense. I fully expected any spirit to begin to rebel by throwing something at me but I felt that this one like all the rest before them was hiding from me. I grew tired over the amount of cases I received with each demon having to hide but yet enjoyed it out of vengeance for what happen to me that night in November so long ago. I hated it at the same time because I had to search for them to find them and cast them out.

The mother looked at me and asked how I knew. I told the mother and the daughter that I would tell them how I knew but I wanted to do something first. I looked at the mother and asked her if she could hear the spirit now. She replied that if she tried she could. I asked her to listen to him while I ask him questions. I asked the spirit who he was. The mother replied that he said he was the boy who passed away. However, I knew better. I knew from experience that demons like to pose as people who passed away and human spirits, if there are any, don't possess people. The devil spent thousands of years perfecting his art of deception, and it has been so well thought out that paranormal investigators have been sucked into it believing that there are human spirits when actually it is a demonic deception. I proved it to one paranormal group when I let a spirit talk to them until I invoked my authority in Jesus name. The spirit became angry and revealed it's true self. Frankly the group was shocked and became believers in what the Bible says about where humans go when they die; either heaven or hell. I began to be known in the community as an exposer of demonic deception which made a lot of paranormal groups upset but I began to receive emails and phone calls thanking me and that they were now believers that what they thought was a human spirit was actually a spirit of deception.

I talked alone with the spirit treating it as a human spirit while my team and Bob grew interested in the conversation, until I noticed that the mother didn't say "he said" anymore but rather "I". I knew then that the spirit had pushed the mother's consciousness out of the way and began to speak to me on his own free will. I knew then that I had him right where I wanted him. There was a long pause in our conversation. I did this sometimes when I knew I was dealing with a demon out of someone. I knew that if she wasn't possessed she would reply to the pause asking "What next" or "what?". She didn't. She sat there quiet looking around the room like any demon would during an event of possession. I leaned in and asked the mother to look at me eye to eye. She didn't blink. I asked who is this talking to me. The spirit spoke up and told me who he was. I asked a few more questions until he messed up. I asked him if Jesus came in the flesh and he replied that he did not. I paused again and laughed. I then leaned in with a raised eye brow and said. "You're not who you say you are, are you?" A sinister look started to form on the mother's face like an old hag. "You're not the boy who passed away are you?" I asked smiling at the same time. Right before everyone in the room the mother grew a smile and her eyes widened and she began to laugh. The people in the room gasped. I began to laugh along with the demon and smiling. I mentioned to the demon how he should get an "A" for effort in trying to deceive me. "You're good at your deception I can give you that." I said, mentioning to the demon just how much I thought that his deception appeared pretty good and convincing, but he just continued to laugh. I then took authority and asked how many demons were in the mother but the demon didn't reply, he just seemed to gaze at me in wonder. He seemed to be intrigued over my presence in the home as if to say, "The game is on, just try and cast me out." I told the demon how he would have to go and that he would. He finally replied that he wasn't going anywhere and how he liked it there. I commanded him to go down and bring the mother back and he did. The mother came back and didn't know what happen. She couldn't remember anything which tipped me off that it was true possession. I concluded and informed everyone how the demon got in the home. The mother's sexual abuse she received left a legal right out in the open. The daughter used the occult and invited a demon in their lives. The demon claimed the legal right over the mother and the haunting began. I informed the mother what she had to do in order to get her rights back from Satan. Repeating every word I asked her to say, step by step she spoke words renouncing the sexual abuse she received. I also did this with the daughter and she renounced the occult practices she did. The demon now lost its rights over the mother and daughter but experience told me that it wouldn't leave until it got some kind of grip on them again. The mother's sudden illness told me this. I blessed water without her knowledge and gave it to her to drink. She felt sick to her stomach after a while then she began to feel better.

The spirits appeared to be gone for now but I knew they would come back so I prayed in my mind to the Heavenly Father how to cast them out. I received a word that they needed to be baptized. I asked the both of them if they had been baptized and they mentioned that they had not been. I asked them to put in a request with their diocese and they agreed.

A week went by and I called the mother to see how their baptism went. She informed me that their diocese wouldn't baptize them since they had been christened when they were young. I instantly became angry and this wasn't the first time I had to deal with a Catholic diocese over theology. The Catholic's version of baptism by christening wasn't true baptism. The word "baptism" comes from the Greek word "baptizo" which means "immersion". For a person to be truly baptized they needed to be "immersed" under water. Because of the red tape from the Catholic Church I agreed to baptize them myself.

I had good relations with a family in Clare, Michigan who owned a hotel that was founded in the 1920's. They would allow me at a moment's notice to use their pool for baptisms. The mother and daughter agreed to meet me in Clare at the hotel to be baptized. When they arrived they followed my wife and I in the pool and one by one we fully immersed them in the water baptizing them in the name of the Father, the Son, and the Holy Ghost. I was curious from the start over how the Lord would cast out these demons by baptism. I predicted to my wife that the mother and daughter would either vomit in the pool or on the way back home. Mysteriously a pastor was present with his family to witness the baptism and prayed for the mother and daughter. The pastor told me that it was a divine appointment for him.

A few days after the baptism I called the mother to see how things were. My fear was that things would get worse in the home, but the mother informed me that everything was peaceful. However, on the way home after the baptism she informed me that the both of them vomited and heard voices in the back of their SUV. I asked them to describe to me what the voices sounded like and she said that they sounded like pigs squalling. I asked her if she wanted a blessing in her home and she agreed. I arrived the next weekend and began to bless the home with anointing oil over the doors and the windows. They thanked me and I bid them blessings and left. After a month I received an email from the mother informing me that they had moved over in the thumb area of Michigan with her boyfriend and that her and her daughter haven't experienced any haunts. I was glad to hear it and talked with her for a bit until we said our good byes and hung up.

We later had found out that Alma was suddenly experiencing a visit from a group of witches and that the evangelism that Pastor Bill was performing in the city drove them away. We had prevented a principality from entering the city of Alma at that time but things can change. Demons are always seeking out new territory or wanting to move in on old turf. We can only pray that churches are wise enough and willing to hear the Lord to know when the signs of a demonic force is on the rise.

EPILOGUE

My friends at Ohio Research and Banded Spirit (OBRS) invited me to tag along with them on a case in West Virginia. I agreed and traveled to Northern Ohio to meet up with Chris Page, Karlo Zuric, Amy Cobbs and Deb Andres. We traveled to West Virginia and they updated me on the case. A gentleman was experiencing the traditional haunting but the case sounded demonic when I studied it more. I was up for travel and had never been to West Virginia prior to this case. The team seemed to trust me and wanted me to go along with them to spot any demonic activity and bless the home.

As we traveled to West Virginia in Chris' SUV and going through the many gates of the turnpike, we spent much time getting to know each other. Like on many cases I go on with paranormal teams the curiosity of the demonic sprung up and I felt the supernatural tap enter my mind. My knowledge and experience began to pour out of me into their cups. I always felt it was important to educate groups on demons so they would know how to treat them should they have any unwanted encounters.

We arrived at the house in a small town in West Virginia and the team went in and did their interviews. The client showed us photos he took which was great but I always went off third party evidence because client evidence could easily be faked and used against teams and even people like me. All that client evidence does is help teams to know what to look for so they can document it. I was always a supporter of the psychological research method that says that a hypothesis must always come out with the same results when people were testing it. If I felt that a team was lying to me about their findings all I needed to do was call in another team and hoped the findings matched. If they didn't match then I wouldn't help on the case. I was a tough cookie to convince and I liked it that way, not out of pride but for the fact that I didn't want people to lose focus on reality and just jump to conclusions. I felt a sense of insanity about the idea that a case had activity in it without the need of doing hard core research to prove it. ORBS and I were on the same page and I like that and I trusted the folks at ORBS. They were serious about getting the data and helping people. The amount of technology that they had was unmatched by anyone else I've worked with. Seeing what they had put me in a state of Awe.

The investigation began as they set the small house up with so much detection that I was for sure that we were going to capture something on media. The team set up video surveillance and a few investigators at a time went into the house. They captured a few things including what appeared to be a shadow hiding behind me in the basement that peaked out long enough for the team to capture it on video. After the investigation it was my turn. I opened the case to the incense burner. Bells rang out from the burner when I picked it up as the team was watching me prepare. It began to rain and thunder and the droplets in the dark felt like a warm summer's rain. I opened the lid to the burner and the wear of the many past cases that it was in showed. I always tried to keep it clean as possible but with having busy periods it was impossible. I placed the coal in a fire I made from a candle. The coal began to get red hot in the tonged that I held in my hand. I placed the coal in the burner as it crackled, then reached in the bag for a hand full of gloria incense. I said a prayer to myself as I closed my eyes and placed the incense in the burner. More crackling began to sound and the smoke from the incense poured out of every hole in the burner. I made my way to the house as the smoke poured out in the darkness under a small sprinkle of rain. As the rain drops sizzled as they reached the hot burner. Off in the distance lightning and thunder sounded. I walked in and began my prayer of cleansing pushing the smoke into every hole, corner and wedge in the house to make sure there was no hiding place for a demon. When I finished I placed the burner on the garage cement floor and we stood together and watched the storm pass over us. I helped the team pack their things and we traveled back to Ohio. I blessed the team and left for the long journey back to my home state.

As I recall this case, like so many cases before it I met no resistance from the dark forces that plagued these people. There was only one time that I recall when I faced a possession that was beyond my reach. I truly thought when I first started to use my abilities to help others and glorify God that I would meet each case with an intense resistance much like I did with the possession of the woman in the Demonic Network story. I did have a sense of fear that came over me but with each case opening my eyes to God's power and the presence of angels the fear left me. I recall going to Bobby Mackey's Music World and entering the well room by myself hearing a hiss, then a growl and finally audibly told to "get out"; without any fear. I stood my ground and responded, "No!"

As I sat in my house in wonder over why God chose me to do these things and stand in the gap for people victimized by demons a friend of mine had messaged me. It was Jessica, a Jewish friend from California who had traveled to Israel. She needed to get to Israel for spiritual purposes and had informed me that she was sending me something. I asked what it was and she responded that she had some items blessed for me from the Church of the Holy Sepulchre. My mouth dropped as I knew that that church stood on the very ground in which Jesus died on the cross. She knew from our previous conversations when she asked me where I would go if I visited Israel that I wanted to visit the Church of the Holy Sepulchre in Jerusalem. When the package arrived it was like God handing me the full armor of God from Ephesians 6:10-20 to use against the demonic. She had bought me two rosary one from Bethlehem and the other from Jerusalem with soil in it, anointing oil, holy water from the River Jordan, holy incense, and a small wooden cross; all blessed in the Church of the Holy Sepulchre. I would treasure the gifts and use them on cases for their own presence to bring hope, love, and glorify God. I treated them as complete power and with each case that I use them in drew demonic activity away.

Still, I wondered what it was about me. What it was in all the cases in my past that would cause demons to become so frightened of me and frustrated that they couldn't do anything. I sat in my home one day and prayed to God seeking for him to tell me rather than lead me to the answer. God and I's relationship is very odd at times. Rather than answering my prayers directly he would lead me on a path to either obtaining the knowledge I needed or show me my next training session that would lead me to finding my answers. It was very interesting and I still to this day receive divine knowledge about things. Much of the knowledge was during each case that would help to rid the home of a demon. God told me that there was a purpose for demons, that they received their power from the divine Law or what you could say The Ten Commandments. The Law was meant to help us to know what sin is and that the Law led to death (Romans 6:14; Galatians: 3:24). Demons whole purpose was to fulfill the purpose of the law. He also taught me that in Revelation that when Satan and his demons are thrown into the Lake of Fire is due because there would not be any more need for them. Man would finally leave his wicked ways and follow in love and obedience to God.

The knowledge would always flow from God into me as I asked according to John 14:14 what I wanted to know. Truly Psalm 23:1 that little verse that ran through my mind when I was a child was correct. I had made the Lord my Shepherd and I had no need to want because he would provide for me. As Christians we don't need to perform some ritual or rite of exorcism to merely cast out a demon. What God taught me through his Holy Spirit is believe in Him, find out the "purpose" of why the demon is there, remove that purpose and have the people on the case repent and in spiritual authority to tell it to go where God wants it to go. Remove the right of why it is there and tell it to leave with full authority in Jesus name. To obtain spiritual authority a person just has to let the word of God richly dwell in them and believe in Jesus. The key to ekballism is to study the word, not being afraid, working at studying and through that being approved unto God (2 Timothy 2:15).

As for me I discovered one day that God had assigned an angel to me for the purpose of deliverance and to break through the resistance that demons hold onto. I do not have nor seek a relationship with angels but I know the angel assigned to me shows up with me on the darkest cases and together we try to break through the resistance of the demons there. For a long time while on demonic cases I always thought I was alone and that God would show up when he wanted to. I was worried that he would forsake me but he never did. Now I know for certain that the presence of the angel next me was what was driving the demons I encountered to fear and hide.

In the end, I can honestly say that with God's help the Devil was knocked down, beat up and throw out of the ring just by a single phone call. My wife and I fought bitterly to the end against the forces of darkness. We fought depression when we lost loved ones, carried each other when the other wanted to give up, supported the other when the other lost their job. For me personally, I lost a lot in my grandparents, my father, my aunt (father's sister), my uncle (father's brother), my career and finally my church that I built with my bare hands. But that all changed on April 11, 2014, my father's birthday. I asked by the Travel Channel to go to Toledo, Ohio and cast out some demons plaguing people in a home. At first I thought things were turning around for me since I was invited to do an episode for The

Dead Files. I traveled all the way down to Toledo and was put up in a king suite. I then waited patiently for the phone call the following morning from the producer to go to the house so they could film me doing what I do to cast out demons. I was depressed since it was my father's birthday and all the memories of his death came back to haunt me. I doubted in my abilities to be able to cast anything out that day, even doubted in God. I would have to say that moment in that day was the lowest point in my life. "Why was I here?" I thought to myself. "I'm not going to be able to cast out evil in this shape." I immediately prayed to God for strength an encouragement. As I was about to get in my knees at that hotel room bedside my cell phone rang. I was a little angry that someone would interrupt an important prayer; still I decided to pick up my phone. I looked at the caller I.D. and saw that it was my wife. I immediately answered the phone and instantly noticed my wife was crying on the other end. My first impression was that something went wrong at home; facing nothing but tragedy will do that to you. "What's wrong? Do you want me to come home?" I asked my wife. "No." She replied. For a split second I couldn't believe the response but then it all made sense when she continued, "Greg, I'm pregnant." At first I was in disbelief. I asked for reassurance and it was true; she was pregnant. We both cried over the phone and instantly filled with joy. My confidence boosted and my spiritual energy was lite on fire. I was going to be a father. After battling twelve years of infertility being told by doctors that we could only have children through in vitro fertilization or artificial insemination God blessed us with a child. We were about to give up and were planning to adopt a child and raise it as our own, yet we held onto God's leg holding him to his promises and He blessed us. Through all the mess, through all the testing, trials, tribulation, and attacks from the darkness we claimed victory that day. Knowing that we were going to have a child did not just fill the voids in our hearts but also filled my mother's and several other family members. The new church we attended knew of our struggles and after our first trimester we stood up and gave our testimony to a crowd that was awe struck. We continued to give our testimony to people who were struggling or out of faith to lift them up out of the darkness. Through it all we were rewarded for keeping our faith and never moving away from God's word. We firmly stood on God's foundation; the Bible. My wife and I both agreed that we should not keep this story to ourselves but share it with others to lift them up out of the darkness, be a beacon of hope and most importantly to give glory and honor where it is due; to the Lord. Psalm 126[127]:3-5 says, "Lo, sons are a heritage from the Lord, the fruit of the womb a reward. Like arrows in the hand of a warrior are the sons of one's youth. Happy is the man who has his quiver full of them! He shall not be put to shame when he speaks with his enemies in the gate." I now have one arrow in my quiver and you just read what one arrow can do against the devil. Oh! And those demons in Toledo - they never came back in the home after I blessed it in Jesus name.

We ekballists are few but many and we are out there using mere words to pluck out the enemy where ever he is. He can hide in the shadows but not for long until we invoke the angels above to find them, bind them and cast them out. I am an ekballist and follow the most high God and call upon the name of Lord Jesus Christ for the purpose of the great commission to save the lost souls in this celestial war between heaven and hell. Know this; we are out there being living sacrifices taking the abuse that the devil gives us, we get knocked down but we stand up and reveal the glory of God in the last round of the fight. They say that demons can see your scars on your spirit from all the battles you fought against them. With me, after all the crap I went through I think they see spiritual scars that tell them that I don't run from a fight.

With Jesus Christ there is hope for this world.

Glory to God

ADDITIONAL BOOKS BY GP HAGGART

Books shown below are available at Amazon, Barnes & Noble and other online book retailers. Call your local bookstore and ask them to order books by GP Haggart. You can also go to www.ekballist.com for information on upcoming books by GP Haggart.

The God Who is Still Here - Did Jesus exist? Is there evidence for the historical Jesus? Do you have trouble finding Jesus? Are you struggling with atheism, agnosticism or backsliding cause you have questions? The God Who is Still Here, is a booklet by theologian G.P. Haggart that will help you through the tough questions; help you find the answers you seek to find Jesus and to know that God is still here.

How to be a Demonologist – Ever wanted to know how you can be a demonologist? From the author who brought you Mechanics of Demonology and Screech Owl: The Lie Behind Lilith, comes, How to be a Demonologist. Renowned exorcist G.P. Haggart compiles all the information you will need to become a demonologist. In this book you will learn the steps to take to become a preternatural investigator and help clients and churches battle against demonic forces.

What are Jinn? – Have you heard about the Jinn from paranormal investigators who teach about it? Got questions? Confused over what the Jinn are? Theologian and Demonologist GP Haggart compiles an essay that is sure to help you answer your difficult questions about the Jinn.

10 Ways to Overcome Pornography – The internet is littered with pornography and people all over the world are suffering with pornography addiction. Now you or a friend can overcome pornography addiction. Learn 10 ways to overcome this stronghold!

Screech Owl: The Lie Behind Lilith - In August of 2009 while visiting the possessed, exorcist G.P. Haggart and demonologist John Mealer, interrogate a demon. During the interrogation the demon describes the origins of the demonic race. In Screech Owl: The Lie Behind Lilith, pastor and exorcist G.P. Haggart takes the reader through the demonic doctrine of Lilith, the suggested first wife of Adam and queen of the demons. Is Lilith real or is she just a demon? Was she actually Adam's first wife? Do ancient manuscripts actually tell about Lilith? Is Lilith actually in the Bible or is she just a lie made up by demons?

Mechanics of Demonology - G.P. Haggart breaks down the study of demonology for educational purposes. Forward by Demonologist Tracy Bacon. G.P. Haggart tells the story of his first encounter with a demon that propelled him sixteen years later to battle demons and empower victims of demonic haunts. Discover the knowledge needed to confront demons, how to investigate a demonic haunt, how to debunk a demonic haunt, characteristics of demons, the science of possession, the origin and nature of evil, the four theories of the origins of demons, exorcism, diabolical metaphysics and much more.

✝HE

EKBALLIS✝

A Novella

GP HAGGART

Made in the USA
Charleston, SC
25 June 2014